The Great Whale
of Kansas

Richard W. Jennings

This edition is published by special arrangement with Houghton Mifflin Company.

Grateful acknowledgment is made to Houghton Mifflin Company for permission to reprint *The Great Whale of Kansas* by Richard W. Jennings, cover design by Kathy Black. Text copyright © 2001 by Richard W. Jennings; cover design © 2001 by Kathy Black.

Printed in the United States of America

ISBN 10 0-15-365157-1
ISBN 13 978-0-15-365157-1

1 2 3 4 5 6 7 8 9 10   947   17 16 14 13 12 11 10 09 08 07 06

To Helen Walker Ratcliff

The Great Whale
of Kansas

Breaking Ground

My story begins where a sadder story might end —
with the digging of a hole.

It was my eleventh birthday, and, as is the case
with all my birthday celebrations, it was also
Groundhog Day, an occasion that honors a creature
with whom I have more than a holiday in common.
The groundhog, or woodchuck, is a solitary animal
who spends much of his time either digging a hole or
basking in the sunshine by the hole he has dug.

That's me.

I believe there is nothing, absolutely nothing, half
so much worth doing as simply digging a hole. A

hole is an achievement. A great hole is a great achievement.

I was going to dig a great hole.

My parents had given me a pond-building kit for my birthday. They ordered it from a catalog filled with color photographs of water gardens on great European estates.

"It's a complete pond in a single, compact box," they explained, using the exact words printed in the catalog. "It has everything you need." And except for the tools, rocks, plants, fish, accessories, electrical power to the site, and the hole itself, it did. What I found in the box was a small underwater pump, a coil of plastic tubing, and a sheet of thick, black plastic as big as my patio. There was also an instructional videotape in two languages.

Never have I enjoyed a movie so much.

I watched that video over and over again, waiting for the weather to warm up enough to break ground. Every night before going to sleep, I'd put it on and listen to the soothing voice of the narrator describe the "calm, tranquillity, and serenity of a private water garden." In English, and again in French, he spoke of "dreaming dreams" and "soothing the soul." Step by fascinating step, he explained how to create "an escape, a hidden world all your own."

I couldn't wait to get started.

Hour after hour, I assembled and disassembled the pump. I spread the liner across the living room carpet and walked around the edges, imagining that the plastic was water. Using colored pencils and graph paper from school, I drew page after page of miniature ponds with microscopic waterfalls.

When winter at last retreated, I took spray paint to the brittle brown grass of my backyard, a flat, vacant half-acre that sweeps like a savanna to the scrublike grove of spiked, gnarled hedgeapple trees just this side of Brewster Higley Memorial Park. Like a vandal or graffiti artist, I drew overlapping kidney shapes and ovals in intense neon colors until I'd outlined my pond exactly the way I wanted it to be.

From a nearby construction site, I gathered stones for the pond's edge, scores of limestone blocks, their uniformity demonstrating the maximum weight an eager boy can carry.

Finally, one morning it was time to dig.

I approached the task like a starving man at a banquet. This was the day I had trained for! Armed with a brand-new forged-steel shovel — a birthday gift from my aunt Nan — I ripped into the earth with tireless fury, flinging dirt right and left.

As the sun rose in the sky, perspiration fell from my face. The hole grew like a living thing.

By noon, I had created a depression in the earth that looked like the point of impact of a meteorite. The bowl-shaped hole was roughly four feet in diameter, with gently sloping sides nearly two feet deep.

At this rate, I figured, I'll be basking in tranquillity

in no time at all.

But don't count your water gardens until the hole is dug. Few things happen the way you think they will.

A sudden thunderstorm interrupted my work. Boiling across the flat Kansas prairie, it sneaked up on me, announcing its arrival with a deafening crash.

Kaboom!

I knew better than to stay outside with a metal object in my hand when there was lightning in the air. I quickly abandoned the job site.

From the safety of my house, I watched the darkened skies release their pent-up power directly over my backyard. My heart quickened as sheets of rain overflowed the hole, turning my modest work in progress into a scale model of what I hoped it would become — the loveliest body of water in all of Melville.

Melville, Kansas.

If America were a dart board and your dart landed on Melville, you'd be the winner, hands down. That's because Melville is smack dab in the middle of the United States, exactly halfway between the great Atlantic and Pacific Oceans, a place with no coastline, no beach, and no blue ocean views.

It wasn't always like this. In prehistoric times, the spot where Melville sits was submerged beneath a vast inland sea. But over the course of a couple of hundred million years or so, things have a way of changing. Today, luckless Melville is as dry as a bone — the most landlocked city in America.

Clearly, it's a place that could use a few improvements.

The largest body of water in modern Melville is a man-made pond in Higley Park, the state-owned recreation area that borders my backyard. Rectangular in shape, and held within its banks by enormous, quarried limestone rocks, Higley Pond was dug by bulldozers more than fifty years ago as part of a Kansas flood-control plan.

My pond, as I imagined it, although not as big as Higley Pond, would be far more attractive than that aging, government-designed lagoon.

The spring rains that had diverted me from my mission eventually ended, and the sun returned. With my nose pressed against the breakfast room windows, I found myself gazing not at the sparkling natural beauty of an elegant water garden, but at a waterlogged trap of sticky mud.

Reality.

I hate how it keeps getting in the way of my dreams.

No Ordinary Stone

For three consecutive weekends, I was trapped indoors by the inconsiderate rains of spring. It was a dreary, forgettable period in which I kept myself busy by memorizing my pond video, performing household chores, and sorting my extensive collection of Kansas postcards, a hobby I find as interesting as it is affordable.

But all things come to those who wait, even to those who wait impatiently. The first sunny Saturday morning found me once again at work excavating my private pond.

How wonderful to be outdoors, I marveled, bathed in nature's spring perfume, serenaded by the neighborhood birds, and warmed to a regular sweat by the welcome prairie sun! At last, we were getting somewhere!

It was at that precise moment that I heard a harsh metallic CLANK as my shovel shook me from my fingertips all the way to my shoulder blades. A hard, unyielding object was buried in the ground.

I probed the spot with my shovel's tip to try to get some idea of the size of the obstruction. I figured that what I'd struck was a chunk of limestone, common in these parts. Some run pretty big.

While everybody knows that Kansas is flat, few appreciate that it's also tilted, like the bottom of a swimming pool, rising more than four thousand feet to meet the mountains of Colorado. The higher the elevation, it seems, the larger the rocks. Many are the Melvillians who've broken shovels trying to lever boulders from flower beds and lawns.

At a foot in every direction, I continued to meet resistance, as I did at two feet, and again at three feet, and still again at four.

What is this thing, I wondered, *a meteorite?*

Hurriedly, I began removing earth until I'd exposed an area the size of a Frisbee. Brushing away soil with my fingertips, I exposed a rock whose sandpaper surface felt like ordinary limestone. But something about its appearance was different.

The strong Kansas sunlight revealed a wide stripe in the middle of the rock, darker and denser than the salmon-colored stone on both sides.

I got down on my hands and knees to see. The stripe was not only darker than the rock around it, its surface was crisscrossed with tiny lines, as if it had started to shatter when the shovel hit it but somehow had held together after all.

I knew right then and there that this was no ordinary piece of limestone.

What I was looking at was bone!

Hmmm, I thought.

In Kansas, finding a bone buried in the backyard could mean any number of things. But before I would let myself leap to conclusions — my natural inclination — I restrained my imagination with words of wisdom that I'd once received from a well-read Native American friend of mine.

"To solve any mystery," he had advised, "first you must eliminate the obvious. Then, whatever remains is the truth."

Okay, I thought. *Bone in backyard?*

The obvious explanation is the dog did it. But the problem with this theory is that I had no dog. In fact, I had no pets of any description. This was not for want of wishing. The no-pets rule is what happens when you're born to older parents who've indulged two children already — children who've since grown up and moved away.

"Pets get hair all over everything," my mother says.

"And they're a never-ending expense," my father adds.

The only creatures living with me at this time were a few ill-fed but optimistic spiders in my siblings' bedrooms, rooms maintained just as they'd been left behind, with every artifact in place, like miniature museums.

Mine was a mostly empty house. Maybe this is why I'd become so accomplished at amusing myself with my own thoughts, and why people said I was "eleven going on forty."

It wasn't a bone buried by a dog, I was sure of that.

It wasn't the grave of someone's beloved pet.

It wasn't evidence of an unsolved murder in the neighborhood, either. Melville isn't that kind of place, and this wasn't that kind of bone.

This was something bigger. Something older. Something locked in stone.

My mind raced ahead to embrace the possibilities. Even though I've learned that things rarely turn out the way you think they're going to, I can't help getting my hopes up.

But first, the Indian had advised, you must eliminate the obvious.

In Kansas the obvious goes deeper than you might expect. After its lengthy service as a shallow sea, Kansas spent many years as sea-bed ooze baking in the sun. This is a time-tested recipe for sandstone, limestone, and chalk, all of which are rich with fossils. Western Kansas is a paleontologist's paradise. Even in central Kansas, where Melville is, you can hardly put down a shovel without finding a rock that's decorated like a prehistoric birthday cake with tiny fossilized shells. Small potatoes, so to speak, but fossils nevertheless.

Could I have found something just as old but bigger?

I stopped digging. With fossils, it pays to be careful. Just because they're made of stone doesn't mean they're unbreakable.

Miss Whistle, my sixth-grade science teacher, says it's not unusual for prehistoric bones to survive intact for a hundred million years, only to turn to dust when mishandled by some greedy commercial fossil hunter or uninformed rube.

With this in mind, I went to find my father.

He was asleep on the sofa, an open magazine lying

on his stomach like a napkin; his glasses had tumbled to the floor where they were certain to be stepped on. I picked them up and placed them on the coffee table.

"Dad!" I called out in a stage whisper. "Wake up!"

"What!" he said with a start, suddenly raising his head and blinking his eyes. "What is it? What's happened?"

"I think I've found something in the backyard," I announced.

Slowly, like a man assembling the parts of a complicated machine, my father pulled himself together and with obvious irritation followed me outside. Once in the sunlight, his mood lifted.

"Interesting," he said, placing a hand on my shoulder to lower himself into a kneeling position. He squinted at the brown-striped stone just inches from his nose. His pose brought to mind a dog trying to figure out if what he has encountered is a possible meal or just something that smells especially bad.

"Well, it certainly *looks* like bone," my father said. "I wonder how big it is."

"There's only one way to find out," I replied cheerfully. Although not a direct invitation, it was the best that I could do when speaking to my father.

"No question about it," he responded. "Come get me when you're done. I'll be right inside."

He shuffled back into the house to continue his nap.

For the rest of the day, I worked to expose the

surface of the limestone. Using a garden trowel, I dug down an inch or two, then with the whisk broom I'd borrowed from the glove box in my father's car, I carefully swept away the loose dirt. Again and again, I repeated the process.

When my legs began to ache from kneeling too long in one position, I'd stand, stretch, and walk around the ever-expanding hole, wondering what lay buried beneath my feet. All day long I worked, stopping only briefly to eat the sandwich and drink the milk that my mother delivered to the job site. I picnicked beneath the big, gnarled hedgeapple trees that grew like giant weeds beside the fence.

I bit into the soft, slippery bread of a BLT.

"If that's not enough," my mother said, "there's plenty more inside."

All afternoon, my mind raced ahead of the facts. Although what I'd uncovered so far was nothing more than a small section of dull, striped rock, what I imagined were a hundred different outcomes, every one of them extraordinary. Mine are the kind of daydreams in which fame and fortune reside. Only with great force of will was I able to maintain the cautious snail's pace of a real, professional scientist.

Work runs on hope.

By late afternoon, the crater approached the size of my original pond layout. Within this newly formed cavity, I had painstakingly removed and sifted the rocks, dirt, and plentiful earthworms to a depth of approximately three feet. This effort revealed not one but five brown bones locked in limestone in parallel curved lines. So indistinct were their edges, they looked painted on.

Since I hadn't reached the end of any of them, I was unable to determine how long they might be, but as I stood at the excavation's rim to marvel at my handiwork, I could see clearly that each bone was as thick as a baseball bat.

"It's unusual to find bones lined up in a row like this," my father said, startling me as he came up from behind. "I wonder what they could be?"

Stimulated by this unexpected invitation, I could contain my imagination no longer. I pictured a snorting, thundering herd of woolly mammoths sweeping across the flat Kansas prairie through Higley Park into my backyard.

"Do you think they could be tusks?" I asked.

"Five in a row?" he responded. "Seems unlikely."

My father peered into the hole, now covered with shadow. "Anyway," he continued, "if they were tusks, whatever they came from would've been as big as a house."

I turned around and looked up at the rooftop of the two-story wood-frame structure we call home. In the fading sunlight, I could barely make out the distant shape of a starling perched on the edge of the tall brick chimney.

Wow! I thought.

Using limestone rocks as weights and my birthday pond liner for a tarp, I reluctantly called it a day and covered the hole for the night.

Tantalizing Possibilities

Nothing interrupts life quite so thoroughly as school.

Just when you've got some real momentum going, school forces you to drop everything. This includes digging for bones, an activity that on Monday morning I realized I'd have to limit to weekends. The best I could hope to accomplish after school and before chores on weekdays was to dig up some facts. So as soon as the last bell rang, I went to see the smartest man I know.

"It could be anything," Tom White Cloud said. "Petrified wood. A mastodon. Even a beaver."

Tom White Cloud's real name is Tom Macintosh, but he uses the name Tom White Cloud to call attention to his Native American heritage. His store is located across the street from the Melville Courthouse, a ten-minute bicycle ride from my school. Although not a very big place, White Cloud Books carries thousands of new and used books on every subject under the sun. I'd swear that Tom White Cloud has read them all.

"A beaver?" I asked incredulously.

"In prehistoric times, beavers grew to be as big as

modern-day bears," Tom White Cloud explained. "But given our state's history, most likely it's something from the Cretaceous Period."

"The Cretaceous Period?" I repeated.

"Part of the age of dinosaurs," he reminded me. "The time from a hundred and forty-four million years ago to about sixty-four million years ago. Back then, Kansas was teeming with huge, predatory fish and strange, bad-tempered, aquatic reptiles."

As he spoke the words "strange, bad-tempered, aquatic reptiles," he glanced in the direction of Mrs. Quattlebaum, a driver for Kansas Parcel Service, who was using a hand truck to deliver boxes to the back. When I first arrived, she'd been complaining about how heavy Tom White Cloud's shipments always were.

"Do you think it could be an important scientific discovery?" I asked. "I mean, given the size of it?" I was thinking about all the little seashells and sharks' teeth that I'd seen in Melville over the years. The five bones in a row that I'd uncovered in my backyard were no seashells.

"That's hard to say," Tom White Cloud replied. "In a sense, every discovery is important to science, because it all contributes to mankind's knowledge. If it's an unusual discovery, then science can become very interested. But even if it's not rare, if what you've found simply captures the public's imagination, then it can become important in another way. A

14

museum might be interested."

"A museum?" I repeated. "You mean, they'd pay me for it?"

Tom White Cloud laughed. "It all depends on what it is," he said. "But yes, museums do pay for their exhibits. Sometimes, they pay a lot. Last year, a museum in Chicago paid nearly eight million dollars for a T. rex fossil."

"Whew!" I whistled. "That's a lot of money."

I disregarded the lightly scraping chime of the bicycle bell that Tom White Cloud had rigged to his front door. I figured it merely signaled the departure of the crabby Mrs. Quattlebaum. But when I saw Tom White Cloud suddenly pull himself to attention, a goofy grin forming on his face, I turned around to see that it wasn't the Kansas Parcel Service driver exiting the bookstore but my sixth-grade science teacher entering it.

Miss Whistle was bathed in a blaze of sunlight, an intense halo flashing like sheet lightning around her head. The light behind her was so strong that my eyes had to strain to make out her extraordinary smile. Miss Whistle is very pretty. With her thick red-gold hair and her short green spring dress, she stood out from her surroundings like the fiery Kansas wild-flower known as Indian paintbrush. It was not the dress she'd worn all day at school.

"Gentlemen," she greeted us sweetly.

"Penny," Tom White Cloud replied.

Miss Whistle's name is really Joyce, but ever since she was a kid, everyone has called her by her nickname — everyone except her students, of course.

"Am I interrupting?" Miss Whistle asked.

"We were discussing your student's discovery," Tom White Cloud explained.

"Yes," Miss Whistle said, giving me a wink. "He told us all about it today in class. How fascinating!"

"Tom White Cloud thinks it could be valuable," I said.

"Really, Tom?" Miss Whistle repeated. "Valuable?"

"Not so fast," Tom White Cloud said, holding up his hands. "All I said was that some of these discoveries turn out to be worth something, especially to museums."

"I see," Miss Whistle said.

"Unless, of course," Tom White Cloud added as an afterthought, "instead of paying for it, the people who want it simply decide to steal it, like the European settlers did to my land."

"Now, Tom," Miss Whistle admonished, "that was a long time ago. And it wasn't your land, it was your ancestors' land."

"They were planning to leave it to me," Tom White Cloud muttered.

Miss Whistle looked Tom White Cloud squarely in the face. Her green eyes smoldered, her lips quivered, and her skin reddened softly from her cheeks to her throat.

"It's too bad you feel the way you do, Tom," she said, "because, believe it or not, there are some of us who've come to Kansas during the last two hundred years who're actually worth knowing!"

Tom White Cloud did not reply, but he kept his eyes fixed on Miss Whistle, who returned his gaze with the same intensity. The two of them gave the appearance of people engaged in conversation, yet neither one was saying a word. The silence filled the room.

After a polite wait, I could stand it no longer.

"So, how about those museums," I said.

I might as well have been invisible. Tom White Cloud and Miss Whistle were in another world. While waiting for their return, I pondered the subject of museum exhibits.

It doesn't take a lot to attract the interest of museums in Kansas. I have ample evidence organized in shoe boxes in my bedroom closet — my postcard collection. Among these souvenirs are cards from Kansas museums boasting such attractions as the world's biggest ball of twine, the world's biggest concrete prairie dog, the world's biggest collection of barbed wire, and the world's biggest pallasite meteorite. This last one, according to the information printed on the back of the card, is housed in a museum constructed right where the object was found, on the site of the world's biggest hand-dug well.

Frankly, for my discovery, I was hoping for something better.

I started to express this thought but realized it was of no use so long as Tom White Cloud and Miss Whistle continued their silent stare. Was it possible, I wondered, that my teacher and my friend had been abducted by aliens and what I was looking at were only empty shells?

This was getting embarrassing.

The only sounds in the bookstore came from Mrs. Quattlebaum dropping a box to the floor and the soft ticking of a pendulum clock in the corner. I realized it was past time for me to be home.

"I'd better go," I said out loud.

"Oh," Miss Whistle unexpectedly responded, returning at last to earth. She placed her fingertips lightly on my shoulder and smiled. "See you in class tomorrow."

"And keep digging," Tom White Cloud called out as I set off the bell above the bookstore door. "You never know what you'll find!"

A Feathered Friend

The shortest way home from downtown Melville is to cut through Higley Park. This is not the same as saying it is the quickest.

The quickest way home would be to take the same

route the cars do. But the cars can't stop beside the pond in Higley Park and watch the wind make ripples on the surface of the water. They can't close their eyes and listen to the birds, which here, at least, are noisier than people. And because the only way to reach the water's edge is to climb down three neatly arranged, stair-stepped rows of limestone blocks — blocks pockmarked with tiny Cretaceous fossils — the cars never get to see Phil, the Solitary Duck.

Phil is a white domestic duck, the kind you see at petting zoos and farms. He lives free in Higley Pond, where he's been for at least a year — maybe more. He's the only duck there.

On weekends joggers, dog walkers, and other afternoon idlers circling the five hundred paces around the water sometimes will pause to toss him stale bread and crackers. But I'm the only one he can count on for a sandwich. I bring these to him nearly every day after school, because my mother always packs too many in my lunch bag.

Most days I hang around to talk to Phil. For a duck, he's surprisingly attentive. I find that these one-sided conversations help me make the switch from the person I'm required to be at school to the person I'm expected to be at home. It seems the only time I can really be myself is when I'm sitting by the water with Phil.

"I was well on my way to having what I've always wanted," I told him. "A pond of my very own. But now that there's the possibility of getting something I never even thought of having before, I find that I want it, instead. Is this wrong?"

Phil said nothing, which is his customary response, and one that I generally appreciate. It's funny, but if people see you talking to yourself, they think you're crazy. But when they catch you speaking to an animal, that's okay. Everybody does that.

Today, with chores, homework, and the unsolved mystery of the bones in the hole nagging at me, I had to cut the visit short.

"Sorry, Phil," I announced while he gobbled the last of a peanut butter sandwich. "I gotta go."

The duck tucked his hard orange beak into his pillowlike chest and released a low, mournful sound. It was more like what you'd expect to hear from a chicken than a traditional duck quack.

"Buh-aaahk," he said.

Using his short, triangular tail as a rudder, Phil steered into the wind. Without looking back, he paddled quietly to the center of the pond.

His message was not lost on me.

All of sudden, my life was filling up with obligations. I had very little time for friends.

A Threatened Takeover

No sooner had I gotten home than the words of my

pond video came to mind.

"Create your own sanctuary," the soothing narrator had advised. "A private refuge safe from the strife of everyday life. Do it now, for such a space is essential for inner peace."

This wise counsel came to mind the moment I opened my front door.

"You don't understand!" my father was shouting. "Something like this requires experienced professionals with precision equipment, not an eleven-year-old boy with garden tools!"

"It's his project," my mother shot back. "Let him do it his way."

"What's going on?" I asked.

It wasn't that I couldn't figure it out, but I was hoping that my question would get my parents to settle down. People are less likely to misbehave when they realize there's a witness.

"Mrs. Quattlebaum was just here delivering a package," my mother explained. "Somehow, she managed to convince your father that that thing in the backyard is worth money. He wants to call the State Museum to dig it out."

"I can do it!" I protested. "I just need a few dry weekends."

"Look," he said, "let's be honest. At the rate you're going, you'd need a whole year of dry weekends to finish that job. And, no offense, but this calls for someone who knows what he's doing."

"Oh, for goodness' sake," my mother said. "It's a rock!"

"It could be a very valuable rock," my father insisted. "But only if it's handled properly."

"I'll be careful," I said.

"Of course you will," my mother agreed, putting her arm around my shoulders.

When it comes to family arguments, while mothers may fail to grasp every detail, the big picture never escapes them. It's always about proving the father wrong. Could this be nature's way of controlling family size?

"You know what the trouble with this family is?" my father asked, apparently primed to provide the answer.

My mother's reply was an icy glare.

Defeated, my father pressed his lips together into a thin, straight line, shook his head, and left the room.

After a silent supper of grilled cheese sandwiches, I went upstairs intending to do my homework. I wound up looking through postcards instead. Somewhere in all those boxes was information I could use.

I never started out to collect Kansas postcards any more than I started out to dig up bones. It was just one of those things that happened. My family had either money for a vacation or time for one, but never both at once. Whenever summer would roll around, instead of heading for the mountains or the beach the way other families do, we'd just hop in the car and drive around in Kansas.

"There's a lot to be discovered in your own backyard," my father would say — somewhat prophetically, as it turned out.

We'd stop in a small town for lunch or just to look around, and in many of these places, tucked away in a corner, I'd find a rotating rack filled with dusty, colorful postcards. I'd always buy a few to send to relatives or classmates, but it wasn't long before I was keeping them for myself. As my collection grew, I became something of an authority on the peculiarities of Kansas.

What other state points with so much pride to wheat, tornadoes, and the bizarre inhabitants of Oz? Who else offers mementos of funnel clouds flinging cows and houses high into the air, or stone-faced men standing beside mule-drawn wagons overflowing with cabbages as big as boulders? With evidence like this priced at five for a dollar in countless drugstores, gift shops, truck stops, and museums no bigger than a garage, is it any wonder that some people have suggested that Kansas may be a little strange?

I found what I was looking for — a postcard picturing two paleontologists from the State Museum of Natural History. In the picture, they're struggling to lift a massive dinosaur bone. They've got it wrapped in gauze and encased in plaster, just like a broken leg, which, as a matter of fact, it is. They're dressed like hunters on safari, wearing khaki shorts, khaki shirts, and broad-brimmed khaki hats. They're looking directly at the camera. With their old-fashioned glasses and strained expressions, the State Museum fossil scientists don't seem like the sort of people who'd enjoy working with a kid.

I made up my mind.

I was going to do this one solo, even if it meant dropping out of school.

Handle with Care

As it happened, dropping out of school wasn't necessary, since a five-day spring break was scheduled for the week ahead. "Solo" may also have been something of an exaggeration. No man is an island, and the same probably applies to boys. While I was prepared to do the digging by myself, I knew I'd have to turn to others for advice.

I could think of no better resource than Tom White Cloud.

"You've certainly got your work cut out for you," he said when, at my invitation, he showed up the next afternoon. "I've visited a number of digs in the Niobrara Chalk Beds, out in western Kansas, and they didn't look anything like this."

"But it can be done, right?" I asked eagerly. "By me, I mean."

"Well," the Indian replied, "that's hard to say."

Using his fingernail, Tom White Cloud scraped the rock and then, to my surprise, touched his finger to his tongue. "It's bone, all right," he announced. "But the limestone surrounding it is unusually dense — nearly as hard as marble."

"I don't mind," I said. "What's a little extra effort?"

"Well," he continued, "there's also the matter of your having to work in a fenced yard around an occupied house. That complicates things, too. It's hard to get heavy equipment in and out."

"I don't need any heavy equipment," I insisted. "I plan just to keep using a shovel and a trowel until it's done."

Tom White Cloud nodded his head. "That may be the best approach," he said, "slow and steady."

He pointed to the blurred edge of one of the five parallel bones. "See this? See how it fades into the rock? A lot of people don't realize that fossils can take many forms, resembling sculptures, carvings, block prints, paintings. This one resembles a watercolor. The bone is being absorbed by the matrix — the material it's buried in. In this case, the matrix is limestone rock, but it must have a high iron content, too. Over time, the mineral molecules have replaced the bone molecules and the object has become unstable. If you cut into it, it could crumble into dust."

"That's not good," I said.

"No," Tom White Cloud agreed. "Still, I've seen delicate fern fronds and complete fish skeletons successfully excavated, and they were more fragile than this. I guess it all just depends."

"Depends on what?" I asked.

"On how big it is," he answered.

The lanky Indian paced all the way around the hole I'd dug, examining the striped limestone from every angle. "It's obviously very large," he concluded, "but since we don't have any idea what it is, it's impossible to say just how far it goes in any direction. There's only one thing you can do."

"What's that?" I asked.

"Keep digging," he replied.

More than half an hour had passed since Tom White Cloud had placed a sign on the door of his bookstore saying BACK IN FIVE MINUTES. And even though the chances of a customer's arriving during that time were slim, he figured he'd better get back, just in case. I thanked him for the house call and shook his hand.

"My pleasure," he said.

While Tom White Cloud's observations might have discouraged a less optimistic person, I took heart in his confirmation that my discovery, whatever it was, was very big.

If ever there's a place to find something of extraordinary size, it's Kansas. In addition to the world's biggest ball of twine, hand-dug well, and pallasite meteorite, Kansans are proud to be home to the world's biggest grain elevator, railroad bridge, limestone sunflower, beef processing plant, natural gas field, salt deposit, buffalo statue, and outdoor concrete municipal swimming pool. Only Big Brutus, a retired mechanical coal shovel weighing some eleven million pounds, is presented as the world's second-largest thing of its kind.

Once again my excitement began to build.

Using a technique described in my science book, I hammered stakes into the ground and stretched out strings, dividing my job site into a checkerboard. Each square was assigned a number. Whenever I'd finish excavating a square, I'd pause to sketch a picture of its contents.

Meanwhile, throughout Melville, Mrs. Quattlebaum, whose job with Kansas Parcel Service requires her to pick up and deliver packages each day, continued to supply her customers with the voluntary bonus service of picking up and delivering the daily gossip. Eventually, thanks to her efforts, a small crowd gathered to watch me work. One afternoon, this included a television crew from *News 2 Kansas*. My father stepped into the backyard to talk to them while they videotaped me digging in the dirt.

That night at supper, my mother, my father, and I dined on potato chips and ham and cheese sandwiches while we watched ourselves on *News 2 Kansas*. The short segment aired near the end of the half-hour program, right after a feature about the South Wind Festival, a celebration honoring the Kansa Indians, for whom the state is named. *Kansa* is a native word meaning "people of the south wind."

It's a mystery to me how TV is supposed to make you famous. Unless you already knew that was me hunched in the hole with my back to you, you'd probably never even realize I was there.

My father, however, had a speaking part. So did a neighbor who was walking his dog when the TV crew arrived. And so did a woman from the State Museum of Natural History, who talked longer than anybody else, even though she'd never set foot in my backyard.

Seated behind a desk piled high with books, papers, and rocks, and sounding like a smart person who does not appreciate being interrupted by people who aren't, the woman from the museum said, "Given its reported location and size, most likely it is a mosasaur."

As she spoke, words appeared beneath her face that identified her as a fossil expert. This was very helpful, because if you didn't know you were watching *News 2 Kansas*, you'd swear it was *The Muppet Show*. The fossil expert was a dead ringer for that theatrical puppet Miss Piggy.

"Mosasaurs were once the most abundant of the marine reptiles," Fossil Expert continued, "until they, like their more famous cousins, the terrestrial dinosaurs, suddenly became extinct, a phenomenon that cleared the way for the rise of mammals. The museum has recovered many excellent mosasaur specimens from this region."

The neighbor, obviously pleased to be on TV, smiled knowingly and said, "I've suspected there was something strange going on there for a long time."

When it was my father's turn, all he got to say was, "You can't tell by looking at it, but Melville is a city that's filled with surprises."

The last words, the TV announcer reserved for himself. "For eons," he intoned, "something extraordinary has rested in peace in an ordinary backyard in Kansas. Soon, it will emerge into a world it could never have imagined. But what is this unidentified creature? What is the mystery of the Melville fossil? Only time will tell."

"I thought I did pretty well," my father said to my mother. "All things considered."

"I wish you'd taken your cap off," my mother said. "It makes your face look too round."

"I thought about that," he replied, "but I was concerned about hat hair."

While my parents were discussing my father's features, I reveled in the attention my project had just received. Me, making news! I can't express how delighted I was.

"Isn't this great?" I said, bouncing up and down in

29

my chair like a little kid.

"Certainly it's interesting," my mother replied politely. "But when it turns out to be nothing more than a bunch of old buffalo bones, what will everybody say then?"

A Chance Encounter

Spring break lasted but a moment. Already, the weekend before school was upon me.

Despite a few setbacks caused by buried rocks and crumbling sides, I'd made satisfactory progress with my digging, nearly doubling the size of the hole. The dark pattern in the limestone seemed to stretch beneath the earth forever. I still couldn't explain what was down there, but it seemed that size was its chief attribute.

As the hole grew, so did my father's anxiety.

"I think it's time to call the State Museum," he said.

Stubbornly, I refused.

"I can do it," I insisted. "I *am* doing it."

Except that this day I wasn't. This day I was giving myself a well-deserved day off. Following a breakfast of fried egg sandwiches, and accompanied by a chorus of meadowlarks and mourning doves, I rode my bicycle to Higley Park.

Arriving at the pond, I claimed a spot on the

uppermost row of limestone boulders that surround the flat, glittering water like theater seats. A copse of river birch and willow trees protected my back. Before me stretched a vista of shiny black paths snaking through a meadow below the earthen dam.

In the distance, an old woman shook her fist at teenage skateboarders. A little girl fell and skinned her knee and ran crying to her mother. Farther away, a woman in a green baseball cap straddled a bicycle in the middle of the path, looking around as if she might be lost.

Being in this spot is sort of like watching documentary television. It's interesting enough to take your mind off your worries, but not so interesting that you can't think about your hopes.

I'd been worried about my discovery. What had started as a personal effort to construct a private pond was becoming something else entirely. I liked the idea of its being something important, but I was uncomfortable with the growing presence of strangers.

I stretched, sighed, and hoped things would turn out for the best.

Restless, my eyes scanned the rocks in front of me for a small flat chip to skip across the pond. Skipping rocks are hard to come by in Kansas, so I settled for a lumpy piece of fossil-pocked limestone instead.

Just as I was swinging my arm back, Phil, the Solitary Duck, paddled into the line of fire. I checked my throw, freezing like a statue.

"I saw your house on TV," a voice behind me spoke, startling me so much that I nearly fell from my perch into the water below. Recovering my balance, I turned to look into the lively green eyes of Miss Whistle. Her red-gold hair was tucked into a green baseball cap. Her arms and shoulders glistened with perspiration. She smelled like honeysuckle at night.

"At least I think it was your house," she teased. "The way the yard was torn up, it might have been a strip mine."

"It's a pretty big mess right now," I agreed.

Holding her bicycle upright between her legs, Miss Whistle removed her cap to capture a strand of hair that had fallen into her face. In the distance, I heard children calling out in play.

"Would you like to ride bikes with me?" I asked impulsively. I gestured to my bicycle leaning against the rocks.

"All right," she agreed. "But how about just once around the water? I'm meeting someone."

This was a pleasant turn of events, I thought. Pedaling at a steady pace, I began to circle the pond, keeping Miss Whistle close behind me. Inside my head, I began singing "Zip-a-dee-do-dah, zip-a-dee-day." Just as I got to the part about "My, oh, my, it's a wonderful day," I ducked to keep from being slapped in the face by the branches of a weeping willow tree. That's when I remembered that things rarely turn out the way you expect them to turn out. It was also when Tom White Cloud showed up on his bicycle.

"How!" he said, holding up his hand. This was Tom White Cloud's way of poking fun at other people's ideas about American Indians.

"Hello, Tom," Miss Whistle replied.

"I just came from the dig," he announced. "High-level bureaucrats are having a big powwow."

"What are you talking about, Tom?" Miss Whistle asked.

"A delegation of officials from the State Museum of Natural History has arrived," Tom White Cloud translated.

"My father must have called them after all," I said. "Maybe they're here to tell us what it is."

"Possibly," he replied. "But as every true American knows all too well, when the government shows up at your doorstep, citizen beware."

Not a Keeper

They weren't at the door, they were in the backyard, and there were only three of them, but having been joined by my mother, my father, and bystanders from around the neighborhood, they added up to a crowd. Huddled together around the hole in the ground listening to a speech, they reminded me of a funeral.

The person doing all the talking was the same person who'd done most of the talking on TV the night before — the woman identified as Fossil Expert.

"As I suspected," she was saying with great authority, "these are the rib bones of a mosasaur. Quite possibly, it is the giant mosasaur, Tylosaurus, marine ruler of the late Cretaceous. This was a fierce, agile, and voracious predator whose only challenger for supremacy of the seas was the giant squid."

One of her assistants reached into his briefcase and pulled out a paper, which he circulated among the crowd. At the top of the page were the words, "The Giant Mosasaur, Tylosaurus. From the Permanent Collection of the State Museum of Natural History." Beneath this was a picture of a big-bellied, crocodile-faced sea dragon calmly biting a giant squid in two.

My first thought on seeing this carnage was, "What big teeth he has!"

"Despite the species' being the biggest of its kind, often reaching over fifty feet in length," Fossil Expert continued as she peered over the edge of the hole, "this particular specimen appears to be somewhat smaller than usual."

Considerably larger than usual herself, Fossil Expert was too big and unsteady on her feet to risk climbing down for a closer look.

"It may come in at about twenty-five feet when all is said and done," she mused. "As mosasaurs go, it's something of a runt."

"Is it rare?" asked one of the neighbors, who, distracted by fidgeting children, had not been paying attention.

"Fossilized mosasaurs are the opposite of rare," Fossil Expert replied, using a tone of voice one usually reserves for the extremely dim-witted. "Hundreds have been found on every continent, plus the island of New Zealand, and more in Kansas than in the rest of the world combined."

"Is it worth any money?" my father asked.

Fossil Expert tilted her head and sniffed, as if the wind from a nearby barnyard had shifted in her direction.

"As to its worth to others, I'm sure I couldn't say," she replied. "But the mosasaur collection of the State Museum of Natural History is complete. We would have no interest in acquiring this one."

"Rats!" my father exclaimed.

"See? What did I tell you?" my mother said to him.

Folding her arms across her ample chest, Fossil Expert glared down her nose and resumed her lecture. Her expression was that of a person plagued by swarms of gnats.

"Permit me to leave you with a final observation," she said. "Some fossils are more easily recovered than others. This one, unfortunately, is not only imprisoned in a dense, brittle matrix, it is also thoroughly mineralized and corroded. Where bone should be, there is primarily rust. What you have here is not so much a fossil as the memory of a fossil."

"So how hard do you think it'll be to get it out of there?" I asked.

Fossil Expert rolled her eyes at the foolishness of my question.

"Try impossible," she said. "For your purposes, that should be close enough."

Digging for More

On television, *News 2 Kansas* teased its evening broadcast with the words "Fabulous fossil find fizzles."

Now everybody in Melville knew.

"I don't get it," I said to Phil, the Solitary Duck, that afternoon. "One minute we're on the verge of a great discovery. The next minute nobody wants to bother with it. But the fact is, they don't even know what it is — at least, not for sure. They're just guessing! And not only that, but most of them are relying on somebody else's guessing. What if it turns out she's wrong? Talk about jumping to conclusions!"

Phil gobbled down the last of my tuna sandwich.

"'Impossible!'" I muttered. "What do they know?"

"*Buh-aaahk,*" he said.

"You're right," I replied. "'Impossible' is for quitters. I'll finish what I started!"

Phil wagged his tuft of tail in approval.

Over the weeks, my backyard had taken on the appearance of a prairie dog village. The grass was just about gone. Fresh dirt was piled everywhere. A south wind played a steady, mournful tune over the rounded mounds. All that was missing were a few rodent sentries.

With trowel in hand, I climbed into the hole where the mosasaur fossil was hidden beneath lengthening shadows. In this light, against the buff-colored limestone that held them, the five parallel bones were a dull, weak black, faded like a favorite T-shirt that's been washed too many times. At their edges, they were fuzzy and indistinct, like thin paint applied to soft, wet paper. This, I reasoned, is what happens when you lie beneath the sea for a hundred million years. Smashed, flattened, and merged, bone and rock had become one.

I tried to figure out which way the creature lay in the ground.

I guessed that the mosasaur's head was opposite the outer curve of its ribs. This would place its backbone somewhere to my right. Keeping this diagram in my head, I carefully scraped away dirt, slowly increasing the length and the number of the ribs. When it became too dark to see, I got a flashlight from the house and continued working.

As I removed the last few million years from the surface of the mosasaur, my thoughts danced with many subjects. School. Miss Whistle. My father. My discovery. Fame.

How strange it is, I thought, *that exciting news can turn sour right before your eyes.* I wished my fossil had never been on TV. This brief flash of fame had been only a distraction.

Layer by layer, one thought uncovered another. I thought about the problems that accompany being famous. I wondered why Kansas has so few famous people — just one former president and a few pioneers — with hardly a handful of postcards among them. The complete list of famous Kansans reads not like a *Who's Who*, but a *Who's That?*

There must be a reason. Either Kansans don't do enough to merit attention, or they've learned to keep their mouths shut when they do.

By bedtime, I'd reached what appeared to be the mosasaur's backbone. It was a long thick section crossing the top of the ribs at right angles, like the intersection of a city street.

Exhausted, I covered up my work and went inside to shower and go to bed. Only then did I realize that I'd neglected to eat supper. My mother, also distracted by recent events, had forgotten to assemble it.

Surprise!

My waking life is divided into two unequal parts.

One part is school, advancing steadily, peacefully, and predictably each weekday, like an atomic clock.

School is not a place where you encounter many surprises, and this is the main thing it has going for it. Its routines are so reliable. Each day, you sit at the same assigned desk. You see the same familiar faces. You eat lunch at exactly the same time. In school, every recess, break, and holiday is mapped out for the entire year. How comforting! And all it costs you is your freedom.

This brings me to the other part of my daily life, the unplanned, unmanaged, unpredictable, frequently boring, and, lately, confusing part. What does it have going for it?

It's the part of life that contains the element of surprise.

On this occasion, I was not to be disappointed. Within a few days, patient excavation of the mosasaur fossil in my backyard revealed not a backbone but five new unidentified bones, also parallel to each other. These were arranged horizontally on top of the first bones I'd found, forming a cross-hatch pattern.

What sort of creature, I wondered, *has two overlapping rows of bones, like the stretched-out loops in a potholder loom?*

Most surprises are sudden, such as when people pop up from behind the sofa to celebrate some unsuspecting victim's birthday. But slower revelations can also be surprising, as the facts begin to come together and the truth finally dawns.

My understanding of the nature of the crisscrossed fossil fell into this second group.

The weather had turned unusually dry. The backyard, once a spacious land of lawn, had been dug and sifted and spread into a barren desert. Meanwhile, the weather pattern that sends air tumbling down the eastern slopes of the Rocky Mountains had produced a persistent high wind that skidded across the flat Kansas plain into the waiting windbreak called Melville, turning my private prehistoric dig into a ghostly cloud of grit.

A real Kansas dust storm was brewing. The kind that turns day into night.

I hurried to secure a tarp over the perplexing bones. *Five go this way. Five go that way. What in the world can it be?*

A mosasaur is a strange reptile, to be sure, according to what I'd been reading. Mosasaurs were big, ugly, mean, and hungry all the time — the undisputed rulers of the mysterious Cretaceous seas. But even a mosasaur's bones must succumb to natural order. They don't go running off in opposite directions.

Do they?

Perhaps it was the flying potato chip package hitting me on the side of the head that did it, or maybe I would eventually have figured it out on my own. But the unexpected slap of cellophane triggered the release of a faint but persistent mental whisper that said the second set of bones were not a mosasaur's at all.

Something else was hiding down there, too!

Classroom Demonstration

"What do an era, a period, and an epoch have in common?"

Miss Whistle had started the day by posing a question to the entire class. Wearing a striped, sleeveless cotton dress, tan canvas shoes, and tiny diamond earrings that sparkled when she turned her head in search of a student with the answer, she looked like someone you might see in a magazine.

Two hands promptly went up, one of them mine.

Miss Whistle chose the one belonging to Mrs. Quattlebaum's unruly son Nathan, no doubt because he was standing in front of me at the time.

"They're all parts of speech!" he announced, speaking, as the chronically mistaken so often do, much too loudly.

Again I raised my hand, this time catching my grateful teacher's eye.

"They're units of measure for geologic time," I corrected. "All time on earth is divided into eras. Eras are divided into periods, and periods, when necessary, are divided into epochs."

"Excellent," Miss Whistle said. "Can you give the class an example?"

"The Mesozoic Era lasted one hundred and sixty million years. As everyone knows," I recited, with silent thanks to Tom White Cloud and a sympathetic grimace in the direction of the now-seated younger Quattlebaum, "this is when the dinosaurs both arrived and departed. This era is divided into three periods, the Triassic, the Jurassic, and the Cretaceous. None of these periods is divided into epochs."

"Thank you," Miss Whistle said sweetly.

From the top of her desk, she picked up a light yellow rock the size of a cheeseburger. Extending a slender arm, she held it aloft for all to see. A thin gold bracelet slid to her elbow.

"Now I'm going to pass this around," Miss Whistle explained. "Please examine it, then pass it along to your neighbor."

When it came my way, I saw that it was rock chalk. Like the much harder form of limestone that I'd been working on in my backyard, it contained a fossil, in this case, an imprint of a tiny leaf.

A fern? A tree? I couldn't tell.

"The rock chalk is from western Kansas, from the Niobrara formation of the Cretaceous system," Miss Whistle explained. "It's made up of millions of shells of single-celled animals called foraminifera. From this fact alone, we know this specimen was once covered by the sea. But what about the leaf? Where did it come from?"

"From a man-eating plant?" Nathan Quattlebaum blurted out.

Hopeful for a better answer, the rest of the class turned their eyes on me.

"I don't know," I said with a shrug, sorry to let them down.

"Let's look at another exhibit," Miss Whistle instructed, lifting a second specimen from her desktop.

Once again I was handed a section of chalk that contained a fossil — this time what appeared to be the footprint of a small bird.

"A leaf and a bird's foot," Miss Whistle explained, "both found in the same general area, preserved in rock composed of microscopic sea creatures. What does this tell us?"

Again the class drew a blank.

"Anyone? No one?" Miss Whistle waited for a reply, but all she got was the sound of shuffling feet.

"Then I will provide the answer," she announced to our great relief. "From evidence such as this, paleontologists conclude that there were islands in the Kansas sea, with trees and birds, and, based on the way this leaf appears to have been eaten, insects, as well. This fossil fragment is sending us a message about our distant past."

It occurred to me that in many ways fossils are like postcards. Unlike the fleeting flashes and fading sounds of radio, television, and computers that go in one eye and out the other, fossils, like postcards, present a single, frozen image that forces you to think about its meaning. It's just too bad that fossils don't have that helpful little paragraph printed on the back.

Miss Whistle returned the fossil specimens to her desk, her face momentarily obscured by the red-gold hair cascading across her cheek.

"Isn't it interesting," she said, summarizing the demonstration, "that even when we hold the facts right in our hands, we must call on our imagination to understand what the facts mean."

The class sat quietly in respectful confusion. Clearly, they'd missed the point. Since I had not, and was the only student with any real-life fossil experience, I rode to my science teacher's rescue by once again extending my hand into the air.

"Yes?" Miss Whistle acknowledged.

"Perhaps if the examples were bigger," I suggested helpfully.

Confusion must be contagious. Her only reply was a quizzical smile that danced across her lips, punctuated by a delicate crinkling of freckled skin at the corners of her eyes.

Oh, well, I thought. *No matter. I don't need to be understood.*

A smile from my science teacher was good enough for me.

A Startling Discovery

The digging is the easy part. The hard part is disposing of what you've dug.

During my first weeks as a solo backyard paleontologist, I used a paint bucket to scoop up the loose dirt, which I then tossed away from the hole to land wherever chance might take it. But as the hole grew wider, this technique proved to be seriously flawed. I found myself removing the same dirt over and over again. So I borrowed a cleaning bucket and some pots and pans from the kitchen, which I lined up beside me. When all of them were full, which was much too often, I climbed out of the hole and carried them one by one to the cedar plank fence that separates my backyard from Higley Park.

Soon, a dirt ramp to nowhere began to take shape. But this method, too, eventually proved tiring. Also, my mother confiscated the containers.

Out of necessity, I wised up and constructed another ramp, this time leading from ground level down to the exposed fossil. I rummaged around in the garage and found the wagon that my parents had once used to pull me around the neighborhood. Years of careless storage had slightly flattened its fat plastic wheels, so the wagon jumped and bumped and rumbled as it rolled, lending a percussion track to my routine of digging, filling, pulling, and dumping.

Steady work pays off. One sunny Sunday afternoon, when I whisked away the accumulated soil and stepped back to gauge my progress, an astonishing sight took shape before my eyes.

My first inclination was to jump up and race into the house shouting an announcement to one and all. But recent experience had taught me that you don't have to blab about everything you know. For the time being, I decided, I'd keep this breakthrough to myself, a secret, hidden underneath an array of brown tarpaulins.

Before wrapping my work, I diagrammed what I'd uncovered, first in pencil and later, in my room, with pen and ink.

The picture that I hid beneath my pillow both amazed and frightened me. More than once, it fathered vivid and disturbing dreams. Amid bones of many sizes going this way and that — some as thin as drinking straws, others as thick as stovepipes — there emerged the terrifying skeleton of a giant human hand!

Connected to a shoulder blade, an upper arm, and an elbow, were a wrist and five long slender fingers! These extended over the bones of the now fully exposed mosasaur. More amazingly, the whole improbable assembly of arm and hand was a staggering forty feet in length!

Who will ever believe this? I wondered.

And whom could I trust with the news?

It Takes Two

As was often the case when I dropped in after school, Tom White Cloud had no other customers in his bookstore.

"That's a lot of bones for one animal," he said when I showed him my drawing.

"Exactly," I agreed.

"First you must eliminate the obvious," he instructed.

"The obvious conclusion is that it's more than one," I said.

"And are you able to rule it out?" he questioned.

"No," I replied.

"Then you must proceed with your hypothesis," he advised. Tom White Cloud looked at my drawing again and nodded his head. "This is excellent work," he said.

"Thank you," I replied. "I was careful not to make mistakes."

"What do you think it is?" he asked.

"I was hoping you could tell me," I replied. "It looks like a hand, an enormous, grasping hand. Look at the fingers!"

"*Hmmm,*" he said. "Have you shown this to Penny?"

"No, why?"

"I'd be interested in her scientific opinion. If it is a hand, the hand seems to have caught itself a mosasaur. Do you know what that means?"

"Not exactly," I said.

"Well, at this point it's just speculation," Tom White Cloud explained, "but that's what hypotheses are — educated guesses waiting to be proved or disproved. Anyway, what you've drawn here could be evidence of a creature that preys on mosasaurs. When you consider that mosasaurs are said to be the biggest, most ferocious creatures ever to inhabit the Cretaceous seas, this poses a very interesting question for science."

"It does?" I said excitedly.

"Think about it," Tom White Cloud instructed. "What ancient beast was capable of capturing a mosasaur?"

"*Hmmm,*" I said. "Nothing that I've ever heard of."

"That's my point," Tom White Cloud replied, tapping his finger against the paper in his hand. "Except for another mosasaur, there's nothing known to science that this could be."

I put my imagination to work.

"Wait a minute!" I cried. "Yes, there is! There is something it could be!"

"What?" Tom White Cloud asked skeptically.

"Look!" I insisted, taking the paper from Tom White Cloud and waving it in the air. "This hand is as big as a minivan! There's only one thing in the world with hands like this! A giant ape!"

Tom White Cloud furrowed his brow. "There's a fine line between offering a hypothesis and jumping to conclusions," he said. "Somehow, an ape doesn't seem likely."

"Why not?" I asked.

"Well, first of all," he replied, "the presence of the mosasaur suggests that the larger creature is a sea creature, not a land creature. Apes are land creatures. And secondly — and you might double-check with Penny on this — I believe that the rise of mammals occurred after the great reptiles all died out; at least, that's what the fossil record suggests. Apes are mammals."

The vision of a great muscular ape engaged in mortal combat with a twisting, snapping mosasaur inspired me to disagree.

"The ape could have lived on an island where he captured mosasaurs in the surf," I contended. "Furthermore, the rise of mammals isn't the same as the origin of mammals, which *did* occur during the age of the dinosaurs. And, finally, this *is* the fossil record! Just because nobody knew about it until now doesn't mean it isn't so."

I folded my arms defiantly across my chest.

Tom White Cloud looked at me and laughed.

"You know," he said with a chuckle, "I'm not sure what kind of scientist you'll turn out to be, but you sure have the makings of a great courtroom lawyer!"

At the Crossroads

Who decides what you're supposed to learn in school each day? How do they know what should occupy your time? Whoever they are, it's obvious that they've forgotten what it's like to be a kid.

All day long I tried to find a way to have a private word with Miss Whistle about my fossil drawing, and all day long I had to suffer through other things instead.

Why do I need to know who discovered the province of Quebec? Or why we say "Celsius" instead of "centigrade"? I had bigger fish to fry. I had prehistoric monsters on my mind!

When the last bell finally set me free, I discovered that Miss Whistle was busy tutoring my hapless classmate Nathan Quattlebaum.

"Come back in half an hour," she suggested.

This was not enough time to go home, get a snack, and return, but it was too much time to be hanging around the hallways in an empty school building. I decided to amuse myself by snooping in other classrooms.

The third-graders seemed to have the right idea. Instead of memorizing useless facts about distant lands like Canada, they were learning all about the place we call home. A postcard on a bulletin board display had caught my eye, a cartoon of a huge, roaring tornado ripping through a tiny farm, blasting barns and bug-eyed animals to kingdom come. Across the top of the swirling black cloud were bright yellow letters that spelled out the words JUST PASSING THROUGH KANSAS.

From down the hall, I heard Nathan Quattlebaum cry out, "I don't get it!"

I shook my head, sighed, and returned to my thoughts. Like tornadoes, most people don't stay long in Kansas; they're just passing through. As the center of the entire country, Kansas is halfway to everywhere else. Whether you're headed east, west, north, or south, Kansas is little more than a place to refuel. It's been like this for a long time. Pioneers, prospectors, Indians following bison herds — all were on the move, with few staying long enough to put down roots. When you consider that in the middle of Kansas is Melville, why, it's a miracle my hometown exists!

Nathan Quattlebaum's frowning face appeared in the doorway. "Miss Whistle sent me to find you," he grumbled. "She says she'll see you now."

And yet, I concluded, as sparsely populated as it is, Kansas clearly has more than its fair share of

Quattlebaums.

"I don't believe your ape theory will hold up," Miss Whistle said when I showed her the drawing I'd shared with Tom White Cloud. "But what you've illustrated here seems equally unlikely."

Whereas most people look sort of sloppy as the day wears on, Miss Whistle was as fresh and as pretty as she'd been when I first saw her that morning.

"What is it then?" I asked.

"I've studied science for many years, but I'm not a paleontologist," Miss Whistle explained. "I really can't be certain what you've found. Honestly, if I didn't know better . . ."

Abruptly, she stopped herself, shook her head, and gently bit her lower lip.

"Maybe if I examined it more closely," she suggested. "Do you mind if I come over sometime?"

Do I! I thought. *You've got to be kidding!*

"Anytime," I said, absent-mindedly stuffing my mosasaur drawing into my back pocket and breaking into a grin that stayed on my face until I fell asleep that night.

"Anytime at all."

Just a Hunch

May is Melville's very best month. The sun shines brightly. The air is warm, breezy, and filled with promise. Flowers flaunt their new, bright blossoms against the prairie sky. Intoxicated by the wonder of it all, the wild creatures emerge from hiding to feed and dance upon the lawns. Only the mournful wail of a distant tornado siren performing its regular, monthly test suggests any imperfection in this temporary Eden.

In the living room, my mother was engaged in conversation with Miss Whistle.

"He's out there every weekend, just digging," my mother said. "That's all he seems to be interested in these days."

"He's very task oriented," Miss Whistle replied. "I can always count on him to finish what he starts."

Her social obligation done, Miss Whistle followed me into the backyard. Dressed in baggy khaki shorts, a white T-shirt with rolled-up sleeves, and white tennis shoes with pink laces, she looked younger than she does in school — almost like a teenager.

I rolled away the tarps that covered the pit.

"Oh, my goodness!" she exclaimed, clapping her palms against her cheeks. "This is fantastic!"

In front of us, in an intricate design resembling Indian sand art, the mosasaur lay revealed in all his glory, from his terrible smiling skull — by itself almost as big as me — to the tip of his bony tail. Marking the monster's twenty-five-foot length were three dozen evenly spaced vertebrae, each as big as a dinner plate, and each with a curved rib bone that descended like a pirate's scimitar.

The doomed killer looked up in hollow-eyed horror from behind skeletal bars, smashed flat and caged forever within the great bony fingers and massive rib bones of some immense unknown beast.

Miss Whistle sat down and pulled her knees to her chin. She motioned for me to sit beside her.

"I can't believe what you've accomplished," she said. "This is truly wonderful! Aren't you excited?"

"I guess so," I said. "I still have a long way to go."

My forearm brushed lightly against hers as we sat together watching the prehistoric picture as if it were a movie at the Metroplex.

After a long silence, she said, "It's not an ape."

"It's not?" I responded, disappointed.

"No," she replied. "I don't understand how it's possible, but it's a whale — a whale that has swallowed a mosasaur."

I was skeptical. Perhaps Miss Whistle knew less about science than Tom White Cloud thought.

"Since when do whales have fingers?" I asked.

"That's a pectoral fin," Miss Whistle explained. She shifted her weight and crossed her legs at the ankles to sit Indian style. "In its bone structure, a whale's pectoral fin — some people call it a flipper — is remarkably similar to a human arm. It has what looks like a shoulder blade, an upper arm, an elbow, a wrist, and five fingers. Not surprisingly, a whale uses its pectoral fins much like we use our hands. Nature likes to share her best ideas."

I'm not sure, but I think Miss Whistle chose that moment to wink at me, although I suppose it could have been just a reflection.

"*Hmmm,*" I said.

"Oh, I can't be positive, you understand," Miss Whistle continued. "With fossils, it's very hard to tell the difference among many reptiles and mammals, especially without seeing the head. In most cases, conclusive identification can be made only by examining the jaw and — if it has any — the teeth."

A gust of wind arrived from the southwest, strong and insistent, lifting the ends of my science teacher's red-gold hair. In the sunlight, it glowed with the richness of prehistoric amber.

"Still," she said in a voice that was soft, soothing, and sure, "what I see here looks more like a whale than anything else."

Miss Whistle turned to me and smiled, her face just inches from my own. Tiny freckles were scattered over the bridge of her nose, sprinkled like the signature of a satisfied artist. Her lips glistened in the sunlight.

I breathed in deeply, drawing the spring air into my lungs and taking with it the honeysuckle scent of my science teacher. Never before had I experienced such an extraordinary sensation. Lightheaded and inwardly trembling, I felt like a balloon filling with a strange invisible gas, leaping into the heavens, where I was sure to burst.

I felt many years older than eleven.

"The only problem," Miss Whistle concluded, "is that the first prehistoric whales didn't arrive until the mosasaurs had been extinct for twenty million years. In the Cretaceous Period, there were no whales. Not a single, solitary one."

I gazed at the fossilized picture of terror from the ancient Kansas sea, a permanently swallowed mosasaur laid out flat as a pancake at the bottom of what had started out to be my pond.

"I'll bet that's what this guy thought, too, right before he got his," I said as my science teacher stood up and brushed the dust from the back of her shorts, and I began the slow descent from cloud nine.

The U.S. Mail

What do you do about something that can't be true but is?

I was sitting on a rock in Higley Park, a wadded-up lunch bag by my side. The sun was bright. The air was clear. The wind was strong, stretching the thin white clouds into strings, like the cheese that clings between a pizza and the pan.

Phil, the Solitary Duck, paced back and forth nearby, quacking noisily at nothing in particular. I tossed him the remains of a tuna salad sandwich that some hours earlier had gone gooey. As Phil settled down to eat, I lay back with my head on my backpack to figure things out.

Before she left my house, Miss Whistle had told me about a sea creature called Basilosaurus, which lived about fifty million years ago. A mammal, not a reptile, Basilosaurus was shaped like a mosasaur, but without a mosasaur's rear paddlelike legs. Basilosaurus propelled itself using flukes at the end of a long, dragonlike tail, moving its lower body not side to side like a fish but up and down like whales. Although many Basilosaurus fossils have been found in North America, Miss Whistle explained, none has ever been found in Kansas.

"It's not that they never existed here," she said. "They probably did. But Kansas has the wrong kind of rocks to prove it. All our surface rocks are Cretaceous. Basilosaurus is from the Eocene Epoch."

Miss Whistle had concluded that the creature that ate the mosasaur in my backyard could not have been Basilosaurus. "Honestly," she said, tracing her fingertips lightly over the surface of the newly exposed fossil, "more than anything else, this resembles the pectoral fin of a modern humpback whale," to which she quickly added, "but that's impossible, of course."

Having run out of food on the rocks, Phil, the Solitary Duck, lowered himself into the water and paddled toward a clump of young cattails, where he disappeared beneath the surface, the white, conical puff of his tail marking the spot where a duck could be found. A pair of red-winged blackbirds paused to watch Phil's antics, safe within a twisted willow tree that years before had struggled through a tiny hairline crack in the limestone. Against all odds, the willow tree defied the facts, broke through the rock, and triumphed.

The facts have many layers, Tom White Cloud once told me. Buried beyond the facts we know, he said, are the facts we don't.

It could be a whale, I thought, but to prove it, I needed help. That's when I remembered Fossil Expert from the State Museum of Natural History. As disagreeable as she was, I reasoned, she'd been absolutely right about the first fossil. It was a twenty-five-foot mosasaur.

I called goodbye to Phil and headed home.

I've always been apprehensive about talking to strangers, even on the phone, so to summon the assistance of Fossil Expert, I picked a method more to my liking — a postcard from my collection. I chose one honoring Chief Wah-Shun-Gah, the last blood chief of the Kansa Indians, whose dapper eagle feather and beaded braids contrasted with his glum expression. I addressed it to Fossil Expert, State Museum of Natural History, Great Plains, Kansas.

Using my neatest cursive handwriting, I wrote on

the back, "The mosasaur you examined was only the tip. Please come back to identify the iceberg." Signing my name and address, I positioned a stamp in the upper right corner and dropped the colorful cardboard messenger into the mailbox.

All I have to do now, I thought, *is wait.*

Maybe it comes from working with fossils, where progress is measured in geologic time, but it didn't bother me that of all the many forms of communication, the one I chose was the slowest. I like the fact that postcards are in no hurry to get to where they're going. I like it that they stop to smell the roses along the way.

Once the die is cast, what's the rush?

The postcard I dispatched to the State Museum of Natural History had no more than twenty miles to travel from my house in Melville, as the duck flies. But how long would the trip take? A day? Three days? A week? More? As *News 2 Kansas* likes to put it, "Only time will tell."

This suited me just fine.

A Wrong Step

Few people have been to the surface of the moon, but thanks to them, everybody knows that it's a dusty, mountainous place with holes, a foreign and lonely place where the only sign of life is oneself.

Did I say the moon?

I meant my backyard.

In my pond video, when the announcer reads the instructions, he talks only about the hole. Never once does he mention the hills of dirt and rock that grow higher with each passing shovelful. But what comes out must go up. I was soon surrounded by a spiral-shaped mountain range of my own creation.

It was a very private place.

The creature that I was freeing from the clutches of time grew bigger every weekend. The forty-foot pectoral fin was joined by rows of bones as big as roof beams, a sofa-size picture for people with sofas the size of shoe stores. But even as I enlarged the evidence, I still wondered, *How can this be a whale?*

No doubt at Miss Whistle's suggestion, Tom White Cloud presented me with a book about modern whales, earth's largest living creatures.

Blue whales are the biggest, the book said, at a hundred feet or so, and can weigh as much as all the residents of a small Kansas town. Humpback whales have the longest pectoral fins, at fifteen feet, fully one-third of their overall length. Sperm whales, which feed on the giant squid, have nature's biggest brains. According to science, none of these whales lived before the Tertiary Period, the period that we're living in now.

But what if the whale in my backyard was an entirely new species?

There's a lot that science doesn't know. Miss Whistle says that of all the forms of matter in the universe, only about three percent is known to man. On just this one planet, there are ten million different forms of life — far too many for anyone to catalog and understand.

Miss Whistle had called my fossil impossible, but even as she did so, we sat shoulder to shoulder looking at it with our very own eyes.

Not impossible. Merely unlikely. As is everything that's one of a kind.

A Cretaceous whale is no more improbable than Phil, the Solitary Duck. That no one's ever seen such a thing before shouldn't be surprising. Every new fact must have its moment of discovery. Until I came along, no one had ever heard of me. Yet here I am.

"Are you hiding back there?" A voice called out from far away. It was my father looking for me.

"Over here!" I shouted.

"Keep talking so I can find you," he called.

"This way!" I replied. "Down in the pit!"

"It's like the Badlands back here!" he cried.

"Head toward the fence, and then turn right!" I shouted, scrambling out of the hole and up the side of one of the many new mountains of freshly dug dirt and rock.

"Oh, there you are," he said above me, his face suddenly appearing on the horizon like the rising moon.

"What's up?" I asked.

"Listen, I was just wondering," he said, beginning a phrase that would forever remain a fragment, for as my father spoke, his leather-soled loafers suddenly slipped on a trowel that I'd carelessly tossed onto the loose soil. In less time than it takes to shout "Watch out!" he tumbled head over heels past me into the pit. With a single drawn-out *"Aaaaaaahhh!"* followed by an uncomfortably loud thwack, he landed on his back on the ribs of the mosasaur.

My father made a strange and pitiful sight. With a dreamy smile on his ashen face and his arms outstretched like a martyred saint, he lay motionless within the petrified belly of an ancient beast that in turn was in the belly of another beast — one unfortunate soul within another within another, like Chinese boxes. His eyes were lost to view, obscured behind cartoon Xs formed when the lenses of his glasses shattered.

"Dad!" I shouted, leaping into the hole. "Are you all right?"

At that moment, a shadow fell across us both as an unexpected cloud arrived, swallowing the light of the sun. With no further warning, rain began to fall, and this, as it turned out, was good news for my father. Like a bucket of cold water thrown on his face, the pelting drops revived him.

"What?" he said. "What is it?"

In reply, lightning ripped across the sky and hail

the size of hard-boiled eggs began to clatter down around us, announcing a storm as fierce as any I've seen. With steadily increasing force, the wind whipped over the surface of the hole, sending a branch as big as a mosasaur crashing down from a hedgeapple tree. Crouched over the Cretaceous rock record, my father and I groaned in unison when from high atop a creosote-soaked pole in Higley Park, the tornado siren burst into a familiar and frightening wail.

Welcome to Kansas!

My father and I lay in the hole, hunkered down like prairie dogs, listening to the shrieks of the wind-and-siren duet.

Then, as suddenly as it had arrived, the storm seemed to go away. A peculiar odor, like that of escaping gas, hung in the air. I coughed, rubbed my eyes, and stood up to see what was going on. Clouds were swirling in circles high over my head, forming a long, dark tunnel leading to the sky. Lightning illuminated its twisting interior, flashing in steady repetition like photographers surrounding a movie star. A screaming noise pressed down on my ears, drowning out every other sound except my father's voice.

"Get down!" he screamed, tackling me behind the knees.

Together, we collapsed back into the safety of my fossil excavation, just as what must have been a

Burlington Northern Santa Fe freight train crossed overhead.

The Other Side

It's funny how even the simplest of tasks, like digging a hole, can be sent awry by sudden, unexpected events.

"Wow!" I said to my father, marveling at the quick succession of his near-fatal accident with that near-fatal storm. "What else can go wrong?"

"Bad luck comes in threes," he replied with foreboding.

I dismissed his gloomy remark with the knowledge that he was still dizzy from the blow to his head.

"Maybe what just happened wasn't bad luck," I said cheerfully. "Maybe it's good luck that I found this fossil. Maybe we owe these ancient creatures our lives, because if we hadn't been with them in this hole, that storm surely would've gotten us."

"If you hadn't been digging this hole in the first place," my father retorted, giving me a boost up the hillside, "we wouldn't have been out here in the storm."

Trapped in the pit, he sent me to fetch a ladder. Although the sun was out, the mountainous landscape had turned to mud, a substance at once sticky and slippery. At first, when I tried to climb the hills above the hole, even with his assistance, I could get no traction. Again and again, I slid back, my feet becoming progressively encased and heavy. But when in one especially gooey spot I found myself completely stuck, I resolved my dilemma by taking off my shoes. From then on, the going was much easier, until, like a sure-footed Indian pony slogging through the mud, I was moving at an impressive clip.

My father's comment about bad luck amused me. Personally, I don't believe in superstition. That is, I didn't until I rounded the corner and careened into a massive padded object that stopped me dead in my tracks and sent me ricocheting into the mud with an open-mouthed *"Ooooof!"*

I caught my breath, wiped my face, and looked up to see the potato-shaped Fossil Expert blocking out the sky. Standing on each side of her, like bookends holding a comprehensive one-volume encyclopedia, were her assistants.

"I was invited," Fossil Expert said, briskly waving my Chief Wah-Shun-Gah postcard back and forth in front of her face like a fan. "And the door was open." She appeared unfazed by our collision.

"I have to get something from the house," I gasped. "My father — "

But Fossil Expert interrupted before I could explain.

"That's okay, we know the way," she said. She stumbled forward on high-heeled shoes into the gummy minefield of my backyard. Had it not been for the two black-suited assistants repeatedly extracting her with a sound like twin toilet plungers, Fossil Expert would've had no chance of getting there.

Oh, well, I thought. *I can't worry about them right now.*

On the return trip, holding a stepladder with both arms above my head, I once again encountered the surprise visitor and her entourage, stumbling, sliding, and muttering as they made their way toward the excavation.

"No time to lose," I called, passing them by.

My father and my fossil had seen better days. Pale and unsteady, my father seemed bewildered as he silently climbed up from the pit, while below us, the fossil looked as if it had been visited by vandals. Limbs and leaves and branches were scattered everywhere. Streaks of mud marred the mosasaur's horror-struck face. Near its tail, and still within the other creature's giant hand or flipper, a puddle had formed in which a pair of water skimmers were inscribing interlocking circles. It was a strangely peaceful picture of nature's wrath and quiet aftermath, until, reflected in the sunlight, there appeared the broad, perspiring face of Fossil Expert.

"Extraordinary!" she snorted appreciatively. "Simply extraordinary!"

"Hello," I replied. "Sorry I couldn't . . ."

"This may truly be a first," Fossil Expert continued, ignoring me. "But the only way to be sure is to uncover the skull."

"Where do we find the skull?" one of her colleagues asked.

"In that direction," she replied, pointing from her precarious position on the muddy mountaintop in the direction of the fence.

Like spectators following the fuzzy yellow ball at a tennis match, the audience on the makeshift mountain turned as one. The fence that my father had installed so many years before completely enclosed the backyard. Made of four-foot cedar planks, it had open spaces between each board so as not to block the view of Higley Park.

"Just how big is this thing?" the curious assistant inquired.

"Well," Fossil Expert said, contorting her puffy features into an imitation of a pig with a persimmon, "that's an interesting question."

Fossil Expert began lumbering over the mounds of mud toward the gate. Her assistants scrambled along beside her, stopping frequently to pick her up or pull her free. As she advanced, she counted out her paces.

"One, two, three, four, five, six, seven!"

I found myself falling in line behind her, like a mesmerized child of Hamelin blindly following the lead of the piper. When Fossil Expert reached the hedgeapple trees at the property line, she stopped and, after a brief spell of huffing and puffing, grimaced.

"Should be right over there," she announced, wagging a fleshy finger toward the gate, "in Higley Park."

The first assistant whistled in amazement. So did I. The expert from the State Museum of Natural History had just suggested that my fossil was bigger than my entire backyard.

"You could be standing on the greatest discovery in the history of modern paleontology," the assistant said.

"Yes," Fossil Expert agreed. "The thought had occurred to me."

Silent until now, the other assistant spoke.

"Higley Park is a state park," he said matter-of-factly. "It belongs to the government."

"That would be me," Fossil Expert replied.

If ever I had doubted that bad luck comes in threes, hearing these three grownups hatch their greedy plot quickly changed my mind.

"Excuse me," I interjected, "but this is *my* backyard."

The museum officials ignored me.

I tried again. "You can't just come in here and take over somebody's private property!" I shouted, turning to my father and adding, "Can they, Dad?"

Instead of answering me, my father slicked his mud-soaked hair over the lump on his head and addressed the delegates from the State Museum in his politest tone of voice.

"What sort of financial arrangements did you have in mind?" he asked.

The Lone Coyote

"That was a close call," Tom White Cloud said.

"I know," I agreed. "They reminded me of a roving pack of jungle beasts. They were looking at those bones as if they were their dinner. I was afraid I might be next."

"I was referring to the tornado," he explained.

The Kansas Parcel Service truck driven by Mrs. Quattlebaum had just pulled away from the curb. With no one else in his bookstore, Tom White Cloud had plenty of time to talk. He came out from behind the counter and settled into a leather chair, accepting one of the sandwiches I offered him.

"Oh, that," I replied. "I thought you meant the museum officials. The tornado missed us by a mile."

"When the subject is tornadoes," Tom White Cloud said, "a mile is much too close for comfort."

The primary tornado, a class-four behemoth with winds in excess of a hundred and fifty miles an hour, had touched down in a wheat field just outside of town, plowing a strip a mile long and a half-mile wide. No one was killed, but six chickens and a golden retriever were missing, according to the wheat farmer. Making the rounds of the TV talk shows the next day, he described how he was picked up near his mailbox and deposited unharmed on his front porch, a hundred yards away.

"Except for the noise, it was a comfortable ride," the farmer — whose name, coincidentally, was Quattlebaum — told *News 2 Kansas*.

Several less-powerful tornadoes were spawned by the big one. One of them — the one I got a good look at — pulled a handful of shingles from our roof and made off with our barbecue grill. But this brush with death didn't concern me as much as the thought that my discovery was in danger.

"What's your father say about the people from the State Museum?" Tom White Cloud inquired.

"He says he thinks they have a 'legitimate scientific interest,' so he's agreed to give them access to our backyard," I replied. "He says they just need to take some measurements, but I'm not convinced. Something tells me not to trust them."

"By 'them,' I take it that you're not just referring to the museum people," Tom White Cloud observed.

"Yeah," I admitted disconsolately. "I can't be sure whose side my father's on."

"That's a tough one," Tom White Cloud said.

"What he doesn't understand," I continued, "is that I don't want strangers coming in and messing with my fossil. I found it, and even though I haven't finished digging it up, I feel responsible for it. That creature and I have spent a lot of time together."

Tom White Cloud nodded. "Everything on earth is connected in some way," he observed. "It's possible that the spirit of this creature is brother to your spirit. With such a force, the passing of time means nothing — not even a hundred million years."

"I suppose," I said. "Or maybe I just don't like seeing defenseless bones get pushed around. This whole thing got started when I tried to build a peaceful, private retreat in my backyard. Now look what's happened! Things never turn out the way you think they're going to!"

"Patience, friend," Tom White Cloud said. "Take comfort in your own words."

The Native American's advice went right over my head.

"If only I could think of a way to stop these people!" I exclaimed. "But it's hopeless. Even my father seems willing to go along with their schemes."

"So, it's all of them against the one of you," Tom White Cloud concluded. "The lone coyote."

In my mind, there appeared the image of a wild dog howling at the prairie moon, but the picture quickly morphed into that of Phil, the Solitary Duck, paddling around in circles in Higley Pond.

"Not a lone coyote," I corrected him. "The way I feel right now is more like a sitting duck."

Up a Tree

For such a sparsely populated state, Kansas sure has a lot of museums — more than states with many times the number of people. You name a subject, no matter how obscure, and somewhere in Kansas there's a museum that celebrates it.

There's the space museum in Hutchinson, the telephone museum in Atchison, the oil patch museum in Russell, the farm tool museum in Bonner Springs, and the shark's-teeth museum in Oakley. And, believe it or not, a woman just down the road is working on a museum to house the world's largest collection of cat whiskers.

But of all the museums in all the towns in this museum-crazy state, none surpasses the State Museum of Natural History in Great Plains. In Kansas, it's number one. This is because it considers everything that's ever existed to be its business.

"Our area of specialization," the official brochure of the State Museum reads, "is all life on the planet since the beginning of time."

Now, their survey of my backyard done, the powerful State Museum of Natural History was noisily setting up shop on the other side of the fence in Higley Park, a park that, like the museum, is owned — lock, stock, and monkey barrel — by the sovereign state of Kansas.

From my breakfast room windows, using binoculars given to me by my parents when my interest was native songbirds, I watched with rising anger as an army assembled. Trucks brought in pumps, backhoes, computers, explosives, folding chairs, and bottled water by the case. A dining tent was set up on the tennis courts. From inside an air-conditioned Winnebago, Fossil Expert emerged flanked by her assistants.

Clambering over the hills of my backyard, I pulled myself up to an inconspicuous spot in the branches of a hedgeapple tree to keep a better eye on the action.

"Not a problem," one assistant was saying to Fossil Expert. "We can do that lying down."

"But most likely, we'll be standing," the other said.

Like a brave patriot whose homeland is overrun by alien forces, I clung to a branch, taking careful inventory of the situation. Tom White Cloud was right. I was facing this challenge alone. While my father cooperated with the enemy, my mother assembled sandwiches, oblivious to the State Museum's hostile fossil-jumping moves. And with summer vacation just around the corner, I was soon to lose my primary fossil adviser and science teacher, Miss Whistle.

What could I do? I was but a lone coyote (a clever one who'd learned to climb trees, to be sure, but nevertheless a vastly outnumbered one). And there they were, my own government, grouped like the Seventh

Cavalry along a High Plains ridge, preparing to launch an assault on my fossil. Things did not look good.

Taking a break from his assigned duties, one of the diggers sipped a cup of coffee and looked in my direction. I don't think that he saw me, but just to be on the safe side, I scrunched down to make myself smaller.

This reminded me of something Miss Whistle had taught the class. Back when the dinosaurs and mosasaurs ruled the world, she said, during the Jurassic and Cretaceous Periods, mammals were among the smallest creatures of all. Not much is known about them, however, since the entire worldwide fossil record of these tiny creatures would fit into your lunch box.

"Some of them were as small as insects," Miss Whistle had explained. "Others were no bigger than modern shrews and mice."

The mammals' peewee size was nature's way of helping them get started in a world where huge, hungry reptiles ruled the earth, the sky, and the seas.

Being big may help you win a fight, I realized, but being small can keep you out of one.

I peeked through the leaves of the hedgeapple tree. The diggers had finished unloading their supplies and were sitting around eating doughnuts. Fossil Expert, I observed, gulped down three.

"Next time get the cream-filled," she instructed an

74

assistant, who jumped at the sound of her voice as if he'd been bitten by a spider.

Fossil Expert's dining habits brought to mind another fact that I'd picked up at school, from a reference book called *Too Fat to Walk: The Story of the Early Whales*. Interestingly, it was published by the State Museum of Natural History and authored by a man named A. J. Quattlebaum, Ph.D.

"Whales arose from terrestrial ancestors during the Paleocene and Eocene Epochs, following the mass extinction of the dinosaurs," Dr. Quattlebaum had written. "Basilosaurus, perhaps the earliest of the whales, sported a landlubber's hind legs in the form of stubby, utterly useless rear fins — proof that it evolved from a land animal."

I found this information discouraging.

If, when mosasaurs swam in the Kansas sea, the mammal ancestors of whales were living on land with bodies little bigger than marbles, then my fossil couldn't possibly be a whale. By now, of course, this was what I dearly wanted it to be. To find a great whale buried in Cretaceous rock in my backyard in Kansas would be a major scientific achievement. It would put me in the natural history books for sure, right alongside Darwin, Crichton, and Dr. Quattlebaum.

I glanced at my watch. If I didn't get a move on, I'd be late for school. I hated leaving my interests unguarded, but what choice did I have?

Reluctantly, I shinnied down the knobby tree trunk, skinning my hands in the process. Just as I was sliding open the patio door, I heard Fossil Expert shouting in the distance.

"Back to work, my boys," she cried, "and there's an ounce of gold for the first one of you to reach the monster's head!"

I'm pretty sure that's what she said.

Unless it was just my imagination.

Ignoring the Facts

Miss Whistle looked especially nice that day. She wore a long dress with buttons from top to bottom. Her red-gold hair was brushed back behind her ears. When she smiled at me, a few of her freckles disappeared into the tiny crinkles that formed beneath her eyes.

"Science is all about facts, right?" I said.

"That's essentially correct," she replied. "Science is about finding factual evidence to prove or disprove our hypotheses."

"Well, what do you do when the facts get in the way?" I asked.

Miss Whistle thought about my question. "If the facts didn't support my hypothesis, and I still believed it to be true," she answered, "then I would simply persevere. I would keep digging until I'd come up with more — hopefully different — facts."

This made perfect sense to me.

For everything that is known, there must have been a time when it wasn't. Every sliver of knowledge that mankind has accumulated almost certainly was acquired the hard way, preceded by a slew of goofball, wrong-headed, and false assumptions that people believed with all their hearts but have since been cast on history's compost heap.

The earth was flat before it was round, a stationary object before it circled the sun, the center of the universe before winding up where it is today, on the outer edge. The history of scientific truth is a history of mistakes.

It was Tom White Cloud, I believe, who said it best.

"In the final analysis," he told me one afternoon in his chronically empty bookstore, "progress depends on our willingness to disregard the facts."

For me, this was easy.

By the time I'd reached the age of eleven, ignoring the facts around me had become my specialty. It was why I had tried to build myself a meditative pond in my backyard. It was why I collected picture postcards with such unlikely and exaggerated images as "jackalopes," "basscats," and Kansans harvesting sweet potatoes the size of redwood logs. It may even have been why I couldn't stop looking at my science teacher at Melville Elementary School.

I wanted the facts of my life to be different from what they were.

I wanted my fossil to be a whale. I wanted it to be the biggest whale in the world.

I kept digging.

On the other side of the fence, the State Museum began doing the same.

It was a contest between two teams, like you see on TV, where the Red Team and the Blue Team compete for prizes. But in this case, the matchup was extremely lopsided.

The State Museum had dozens of members, tons of equipment, unlimited supplies, years of professional experience, and a five-day workweek.

I had nobody but me and few tools, and for the next couple of weeks, at least, I could work only on Saturdays and Sundays.

The odds, it seemed, were in favor of the State Museum. Nevertheless, I figured I had a fighting chance. First of all, I had a big head start. I'd already dug up more than half of my backyard, and by now the job was getting easier. And I had something else going for me, too. Unlike the invaders on the other side of the fence, I was defending my property and my home.

Never underestimate the determination of the native people! I declared to myself.

Of course, no sooner did I have this valiant thought than I remembered Tom White Cloud's ancestors. The European settlers not only took the Native Americans' land, they shot them, they shot their bison, and then, for good measure, they gave them smallpox.

While the State Museum people were digging, I was sidelined by the final weeks of school. When the State Museum people were off enjoying a carefree weekend, I diligently moved dirt, enlarging the crater on my side of the fence. Yielding to this alternating but steady pace, the creature surrounding the grimacing mosasaur continued to expand.

With our on-again, off-again schedules, I saw very little of the State Museum people. I'd hear them setting up as I got ready for school. Sometimes, after I'd finished all my chores, I'd walk over to the fence and watch them pack to leave. After supper, in the golden light before the sun slipped beneath the horizon, I'd cross over and investigate their progress.

For all their numbers and equipment, they weren't especially good at their profession, I thought. Their excavation seemed haphazard, with ditches and disconnected holes dug at random. Whereas I'd been digging steadily from the middle out, the State Museum team appeared to be concentrating on finding the great creature's head. Both of us were making good progress.

I'd nearly reached the fence, creating a rectangular crater almost a hundred feet long and fifty feet wide. It was a great hole, as impressive in its size and shape as a schoolhouse basement. Just looking at it made me very proud.

I did this, I thought. *With my own two hands, I did this!*

The mosasaur acknowledged my achievement with his unrelenting grin. How insignificant a creature he now seemed, permanently framed by the massive, mysterious bones of an unknown, headless, and fish-shaped beast.

Bones are porous. Rocks are not. Fossils fall somewhere in between. Tom White Cloud had explained that water deposits minerals within the pore spaces of the bone, making the bones harder and heavier, more like the rock that holds them. Eventually, he said, it becomes difficult to tell the two materials apart. In Africa, he said, there are fossil bones that have turned into opal.

Imagine, a dinosaur made of semiprecious stone!

More common in this country, he told me, are uranium bones — easier to unearth but radioactive!

What I was working on were iron bones, bones that as the eons passed, had turned to rust within the limestone matrix. Now, about all that distinguished them was their color. They were darker than the surrounding stone, ranging from a dull, dark brown to a deathly gray and black. At the edges of the bone, this color became wispy and faint. I had to admit it was a peculiar-looking fossil.

Honestly, if you didn't know better, you'd swear somebody had simply painted it onto the rock.

A Surprise Gift

Melville Elementary School sits in the middle of a broad flat field of parking lots and prairie grasses, a site it shares with a one-room schoolhouse built in 1876 that today is the home of the Melville Museum of Yarn.

Safety patrol officers conscripted from my own sixth grade stopped the flow of minivans to let me cross. It was the last day of school, and I can't say that I was happy about it. With no vacation planned, my digging nearly done, and all my work in peril from a band of fossil gypsies from the State Museum of Natural History, summer loomed before me like a wilderness.

In my backpack, I carried gifts for my teachers. This was a tradition that to my mother's mind always called for candles — round, perfumed ones for the women, square, spice-scented ones for the men — each one boxed, gift-wrapped, and presented with a signed thank-you card from me.

I participated in this ritual only because my mother insisted. But for my science teacher's gift, I secretly abandoned my mother's unimaginative choice and substituted a carefully selected fossil fragment from my backyard. I chose one that had come loose from where the mosasaur bones began to crisscross with those of its captor.

The fragment fitted easily into a shoebox. To anybody else, this little discolored rock would have seemed worthless. To me, however, it represented something that Miss Whistle and I had in common, something special.

I had wrapped it in floral paper with a yellow bow. On an accompanying card, in my neatest handwriting, I signed my name underneath the single adverb "Fondly."

I don't know how she does it, but Miss Whistle never seems to wear the same clothes twice. This time she was dressed in a gold cotton sweater and a pleated skirt that reached her ankles. The outfit focused attention on her face, and her face once again was smiling at me.

"Why, thank you," she said. "Shall I open it now?"

"I guess so," I replied.

"Then perhaps while I'm doing that, you'd like to open this," she said, handing me a gift-wrapped box so light I thought it might be empty. Smaller than a book, it was as light as a feather from Phil.

"You didn't have to get me a present," I said.

"Just open it," Miss Whistle insisted.

Beneath the box lid, folds of white tissue paper

concealed the surprise within. Eagerly, I parted them to reveal an antique black-and-white postcard. The scene was of two men and a boy at a river, struggling to land a fish. One man was in the water with a pole. The other man and the boy were on the bank, pulling on a rope. The fish, a largemouth bass with a hook in its upper lip, was bigger than the boy, and bigger, too, than either of the men.

At the top of the postcard was printed, "Landing a Good One." At the bottom it said, "Copyright 1910 Martin Post Card Company."

"It's a Dad Martin!" I cried.

What I held in my hand was one of the best examples of the American fish story, the legend of the whopper, presented in a seamlessly doctored image by the most popular Kansas photographer of his day. His clever photo exaggerations are much prized by postcard collectors.

"Someone told me that you like these," Miss Whistle said.

"But these are impossible to find!" I exclaimed.

"Not impossible." She laughed, giving me a wink. "Merely unlikely."

All of a sudden I was embarrassed. Here was Miss Whistle giving me something valuable, and all I was offering in return was a stupid rock.

I wished I hadn't been so quick to swap my mother's candle.

"Is this what I think it is?" Miss Whistle asked as

she examined the flat, drab slab of native stone.

"Uh, I guess so," I said. "What do you think it is?"

"From your discovery?" she said. "You're sharing it with me?"

"Uh-huh," I replied.

"How generous of you!" she said. "I know just what I'll do with it!"

I took the long way home, through Higley Park. My backpack was stuffed to breaking with the contents from my desk. I stopped by the pond to rest and to look at my present.

Martin wasn't the only tall-tale postcard publisher in America's early days, but there's no doubt he was the best. His attention to detail makes you think his pictures are real, even though you know what you're looking at is a phony. Such skillful illusions were considered fun by both the trickster and the tricked, and in those days in Kansas, there wasn't a lot of fun to be found.

Tom White Cloud says that most of the early settlers were people who'd been bamboozled by the railroads. The big railroads wanted to populate the prairie with obedient, hard-working white people so the troublesome Indians would pack up and leave. But instead of the heaven on earth the railroads promised, the early Kansans found a life of drudgery, hardship, and isolation.

Enter professional pranksters like Dad Martin. In

a disillusioned land, a story that makes you smile is worth every penny of the nickel that it costs.

I lay back on the rocks.

Melville was enjoying the best weather it was going to get all year. Above me, clouds puffed up and floated in place like tethered balloons. In the trees, songbirds were holding an all-day concert. Nearby, brown rabbits took up positions in the soft, green grass, like outfielders waiting for a turn at bat. And unless my eyes were playing tricks on me, deep in the shadow of a jasmine bush, roosting as if it were the middle of the night, were half a dozen black-and-white chickens.

I would have lain like this for hours, just basking in the sparkle of the water, but suddenly Phil began complaining noisily.

I jumped up to see the duck paddling in frantic zigzags, an unattended golden retriever nipping at his tail.

"Hey!" I shouted, sounding the best whistle I could produce. "You cut that out!"

Reluctantly, the wayward dog gave up, returned to shore, and trotted off to pursue other sport.

"What's the world coming to," I muttered, "when a duck isn't safe in his own pond?"

It's unusual for dogs to be on the loose in Higley Park. Park rules prohibit it. So does common sense. I scanned the horizon to see if I could spot the dripping outlaw's owner. That's when I saw a crowd of people heading in the direction of my house.

What now? I wondered.

Scientific Breakthrough

Half the population of Melville, it seemed, was gathered at the fossil site. On the park side of the fence, the dig resembled a gypsy camp. Common lunch-box litter lay on mounds of freshly dug dirt. Tents, trailers, and trucks ringed a swimming pool-size excavation. At one end, separated by a thick manila rope, were bleachers dragged from Higley Park's baseball fields. Every available seat was filled with noisy Melvillians.

In front of this gallery was a squat platform perhaps four feet high. Smaller than a bandstand, it seemed better suited as a high lookout tower for a shrubbery farm. Nevertheless, Fossil Expert, her assistants, and the *News 2 Kansas* video team were all shoved together on the flimsy minideck.

Raising his hands for attention, one of the assistants addressed the crowd.

"Before we remove the last layer of dirt covering the fossil," he announced, "permit me to introduce the fossil expert without whom none of this would have been possible."

A handful of Melvillians responded with restrained

applause.

Fossil Expert squeezed out from the center of the platform and waved to the crowd as if she were the president of the United States of America.

Good grief! I thought.

Gripping the handrail tightly, she stumbled down the platform's short stairs and descended into a pit that extended all the way to my backyard. Only a narrow dirt wall, not two feet wide, separated the State Museum's dig in Higley Park from my half of the excavation. Clinging precariously atop this flimsy divide was the cedar plank fence.

For only the second time in a hundred million years, my mosasaur was about to see his captor's head.

"In an unparalleled paleontological achievement from your State Museum of Natural History," Fossil Expert bellowed, "I now unveil the greatest reptile ever to inhabit the earth."

Reptile? I thought. *No way! For a person so challenged by gravity, this woman sure does jump to a lot of conclusions!*

Using a whisk broom, Fossil Expert began brushing away the last few millimeters of dirt. Clouds of dust flew high into the air. Coughing loudly, she continued. Soon the air was so thick you couldn't see anything except the shadowy figure of a big woman with a little broom, bent over like an umpire at home plate. Minutes ticked by until a quarter-hour passed.

The crowd became impatient.

"This is not working," Fossil Expert called from inside her personal cloud. "We need a Shop-Vac for this job."

A dinosaur digger took off for one of the trailers, quickly returning with a fat orange vacuum cleaner attached to a long extension cord.

"Fire it up!" Fossil Expert ordered.

The machine roared to life.

With hired help finishing the job, Fossil Expert paused to catch her breath. Her face was covered with grime. Her clothing was coated with dust. She looked not so much like an almost-famous paleontologist as a common chimney sweep.

"I can see it now!" she shrieked above the blast of the Shop-Vac. "It's the skull! What a beauty!"

The crowd of Melvillians gasped its approval. This was the spectacle it had come to see. From the platform above, the camera crew sprang into action.

There was plenty for *News 2 Kansas* to photograph. From head to tail, subdivided by a thin dirt wall, the beast was easily one hundred twenty feet in length, twenty-five feet of which was the great fossil skull. The ancient creature lay on his side, neatly flattened, as if he'd been run over by a Denver-bound truck on Interstate 70 and left to dry in the hot prairie sun.

Small children cried out in fear. Adults fired snapshots like hunters reduced to using their pistols. Dogs barked, including the golden retriever who'd hassled Phil at Higley Pond.

It was, without a doubt, the single biggest thing that Melville, Kansas, had ever seen.

"What is it?" shouted Mrs. Quattlebaum. "Some sort of sea monster?" Though in uniform and on duty, she, too, had been standing idly by.

Fossil Expert held up her hand, an unmistakable command for silence.

"Positive identification could take weeks," she sputtered in her most officious manner. "However, I will conduct a preliminary examination. Please step back."

The state's largest living appointed official squatted down, dwarfed by the dead sea creature's huge jawbone.

"That's strange," she said.

"What's strange?" Mrs. Quattlebaum said.

"The jaw hinge is not that of a reptile," Fossil Expert replied.

"So?" Mrs. Quattlebaum said. "Is that a problem?"

"This is the jaw hinge of a mammal," Fossil Expert declared. "So are the teeth and the bones of the inner ear. The cheekbone arch beneath the eyes is typical of mammals. From such evidence, one must conclude that this is — or was — a mammal."

Having wished for earth's largest mammal ever since Miss Whistle had first suggested the possibility, I cried out, "All right!"

Fossil Expert ignored my outburst.

With *News 2 Kansas* recording her every word, she continued, "Even more peculiar, the entire skeletal structure is similar to that of modern whales, though what we have here suggests several different species within a single specimen. Remarkably, this fossil possesses the head of a sperm whale, the fins of a humpback, and is bigger than the biggest blue whale ever known."

"Yesss!" I cried, pumping my hand in the air.

Fossil Expert stood and faced the cameras and the crowd.

"Something is going on here," she said. "There are suspicious aspects to this fossil that don't fit what we know about the period. It may look like a whale, but frankly, something's fishy."

"How interesting," Mrs. Quattlebaum observed.

"For such a creature to have lived at all ridicules modern science," Fossil Expert concluded. "For it to be fossilized within Cretaceous rock is impossible."

Staring menacingly in my direction, the mountainous fossil scientist wagged her substantial finger in the air. "Someone is pulling my leg," she said, conjuring up an image that I would never, not in a lifetime, have pictured on my own.

Then, like an ocean liner changing course, Fossil Expert turned away from me and spoke to the twice-astonished crowd the fateful words that would turn my life upside down.

"This fossil," she declared, "is a fake!"

Falsely Accused

If you've ever had someone yell at you, you know how bad that can make you feel. But hearing words shouted in anger aren't as awful as being whispered about.

Whispers begin like mist, a nearly invisible fog drifting in from many different directions, loosely united particles of pure coincidence, circumstantial evidence, fuzzy thinking, wrong-headed opinion, ignorant superstition, and bad intentions — all mixed and blended in empty heads until there's so much of it, nobody can see the truth.

They thought I did it. They thought I'd painted the fossil picture on the limestone and covered it up with dirt and rock. And it didn't help my case that Nathan Quattlebaum went around showing everyone my drawing.

"It's his preliminary sketch," my classmate claimed. "The one he made before he painted the fossil actual size. I found it when he dropped it in the hallway at school."

Wherever I went, people stopped what they were doing, looked at me, and whispered.

"Psst! Psst! Psst!" I heard them saying.

Translated, this means, "There he is! That's the one!"

Even on TV, although they never mentioned my name, *News 2 Kansas* presented me as someone who was up to no good. When Fossil Expert wagged her finger at the crowd, saying, "Someone is pulling my leg," the camera cut to my unsmiling face.

"The motive here is simple," the announcer said. "Greed. Fossil fakes can bring their so-called discoverers untold riches. But here, counterfeiters who get caught can expect to pay a heavy price. The laws against fossil fraud in Kansas are the strictest in the nation!"

I gulped when I heard this news. All those weeks of digging, only to be falsely accused! The thought sent shivers down my spine and pricked two tiny tears from the corners of my eyes.

I felt powerless.

How could I possibly defend myself against a charge like this? And to whom could I offer my defense?

In my mind, I cried, "I'm innocent!" But an imaginary courtroom filled with frowning strangers ignored my pleas and declared, "Guilty as charged!"

Empty minds fill with falsehood, jump to a conclusion, and then snap shut. No one, it seems, takes the time to think. Maybe what they'd decided I'd done wasn't impossible, but I ask you, which is more unlikely, that a kid could find a fossil of a great Cretaceous whale or that he had the artistic skills to forge one?

Following a cold bologna sandwich supper, I went back outside. The evidence of the gypsy diggers was gone — the bleachers, the trailers, the trucks. The job site was a wreck. It looked as if the earth itself had exploded. A few stray sightseers stood at the excavation's edge taking pictures of the monster down below.

In the great divided pit, the mosasaur within the whale remained a startling sight, crying out in a silent scream across a distance more like light-years than the measurements we use to mark our lives. Keeping my distance from the tourists, I found a safe spot to sit down.

It is a whale, I told myself, *but because nobody's ever seen one like this before, they don't believe it's real.*

I closed my eyes.

My science teacher says there are forty species of whales alive today, and another one hundred and forty are extinct. So where is it written that there can't be any more?

I remembered words Tom White Cloud once spoke.

"One man must know the truth," he told me, "before all men can know the truth."

I stood up.

"There are not one hundred and forty extinct whale species," I said to the setting sun. "There are one hundred and forty-one — just as soon as I give this guy a scientific name!"

I looked at the fantastic Goliath in the pit. He was squashed flat and reduced to bone-shaped lines, like a great x-rayed coyote in a *Road Runner* cartoon, his prized mosasaur snack barely past his lips when death stopped him in his tracks. Whales, I knew from recent study, have names that include the Latin word for whale, *cetus*. My whale was the only one ever found in Kansas. His most distinguishing characteristic was his size.

Suddenly, his name was obvious.

"Presenting *Kansascetus humongous*," I announced to a crimson prairie sky, "the Great Whale of Kansas!"

A Tradition of Fraud

"It's a tradition that goes back at least two hundred years," Tom White Cloud explained. "Just this year, a scientific society was embarrassed to admit that the archaeopteryx fossil featured on the cover of its magazine — a specimen for which they'd paid a Chinese peasant eighty thousand dollars — was a complete hoax."

"Gosh," I said, and then I sneezed.

I had ridden my bicycle to White Cloud Books, where I found the Native American owner hard at work dusting his inventory.

"Of course, it was a lot easier in the early days,"

Tom White Cloud continued. "It used to be, all a fossil forger had to do was mix and match any sort of bones to make something good enough to dupe the public out of its cash. This was a favorite trick of a museum owner named Koch back in the nineteenth century. Koch's greatest achievement was a sea serpent one hundred and fourteen feet long, which he'd assembled from the vertebrae of five different Basilosaurus specimens."

"*Hmmm,*" I said. "So how did these people get caught?"

"To tell the truth," Tom White Cloud replied, "a sizable number of them got away with it — at least, they did during their lifetime, which was time enough to enjoy their money. Science didn't really begin to understand the fossil record until modern techniques of analysis were developed. Carbon dating, for example, has brought a number of fakes to light."

"Carbon dating?" I asked.

"All organic materials emit low levels of carbon radiation," Tom White Cloud replied. "This radiation loses its strength at a predictable rate over very long periods of time. By measuring the radiation, you can determine the approximate age of the object."

He removed a book from the shelves, which caused me to sneeze again.

"I wonder how old this dust is," I muttered.

Taking no offense at my remark, Tom White Cloud replied, "This dust may once have been the very first creature ever to set foot on land. It may also have been the bones of the first chief of the Kansa Indians — or the last. It could even have been the wings of an eagle or the claws of a bear. Everything in nature is used again and again. It's the most perfect circle you can imagine."

I nodded my head politely. Sometimes Tom White Cloud strays from the subject being discussed.

"So carbon dating is putting an end to phony fossils, right?" I asked.

"Not at all," he replied. "The fake-fossil business is booming. The difference today is that instead of the fossil hunters making all the money, everybody's in on it — the scientists, the museums, the sponsors, even the ticket-buying public."

"What?" I exclaimed. "I don't understand."

"These days, many of the fossils on display have plastic parts," he said. "Especially the big ones, like dinosaurs, mastodons, and prehistoric whales. Sometimes these fake pieces fill in for missing bones or parts. Sometimes they're used because the real fossilized bone is too fragile or too heavy to display. But a few of the most popular exhibits in museums today, including a few at the State Museum of Natural History, don't contain a single ounce of authentic fossil. They're nothing but plastic repro- ductions."

"You mean models, like you'd find in hobby stores?" I asked.

"That's right," Tom White Cloud said. "And the strange thing is, nobody seems to mind."

"Well, I'll be," I replied. "I never knew they did that."

"Well, now you do," the Indian said, chuckling. "Yet another circumstance where the facts aren't what they appear to be."

"Yeah," I muttered. "Like everybody thinking I faked my whale."

"Not everybody," he corrected. "Plenty of people are on your side. They're just not the noisy ones. Anyway, keep your chin up. This could all turn out to your advantage."

"How do you figure?" I asked.

"Indian history," he replied mysteriously.

Before I could extract an explanation, a man from the courthouse across the street walked in asking about a hard-to-find book of Kansas songs and songwriters.

Tom White Cloud happily abandoned his housekeeping. It wasn't every day his bookstore had a real live customer.

Art Lessons

Reality. What a nuisance!

Could it be that the reason something doesn't turn out the way we expect it to is that we let it happen?

Or are we powerless, once events get out of hand?

Melville's first reaction to Fossil Expert's charges were surprising enough. What happened next was downright astonishing.

I'd returned to the scene of the so-called crime, resolved to make a few improvements. With a little effort, I figured, I could construct a pathway around the fossil that would provide an excellent view of the Great Whale of Kansas from every angle. Under other circumstances, such work might have been tedious, but on this occasion, I was delighted by a surprise visit from Phil, the Solitary Duck, who was possibly avoiding his dog.

While I worked, visitors came and went from the park side of the excavation. The groups were small — mostly twos and threes — and they stood at a respectful distance in silence. Some of them brought cameras, which they used to snap pictures before departing.

"What do you suppose that's all about?" I asked Phil.

The duck squatted in the shadow of a hedgeapple tree, tilted his head to one side, and replied, *"Buh-aaahk!"*

"If you say so," I said.

When it comes to conversation, a duck is every bit as good as a dog. Few people know this. Even as smart a people as the early Indians of Kansas had only dogs to talk to — that is, until the Spanish explorers showed up on horseback. Then the Indians wanted horses, of course.

Things certainly didn't turn out the way they thought they would.

Tom White Cloud said that Indian history could help me, but how? If the history of America's native people proves anything, it's that Indians always lose. And nowhere did Indians lose bigger than in Kansas.

Kansas was the government's holding pen for most of the eastern tribes and the Plains Indians. In my collection, I have a photo postcard of a native family inside a tent — a father, a mother, three children, a baby, and a grandmother — all with faces frozen in fear, as if the camera they were looking at was the barrel of a gun.

From the other side of the fence, just as this recollection was crossing my mind, a stranger pointed a camera in my direction.

Instinctively, I ducked my head.

On the printed part of the Indian family postcard, it says, "For centuries, Kansas was home to many Indian tribes, but in the eighteen hundreds, greedy neighbors, crooked traders, white men's diseases, and a nation at war with itself turned their homeland into a cemetery. In Kansas, the Native American came face-to-face with extinction."

Extinction?

Was this the history that was going to save me? Or was it merely the fate that awaited me, like the dinosaurs, the mosasaurs, and the Great Whale of Kansas?

Something about my whale attracted interest. Across the fence, the crowd had grown. Men, women, and children were gathering in groups of as many as a dozen, peering in astonishment at the incredible sight. Unlike typical tourists, they were assembling quietly, solemnly, respectfully, like pilgrims at a holy shrine. Some even stooped to retrieve their candy wrappers.

My curiosity aroused, I stepped through the cedar gate to join them, with Phil padding close behind.

Beyond the devastated area so recently ripped asunder by professional diggers, Higley Park was entering the full flower of a prairie summer. Yellow wood sorrel and white blooming bindweed grew along the sunny pathways. Queen Anne's lace and partridge pea, with leaves like miniature palm fronds, waved to the south wind in the rolling fields. Milkweed and wild columbine were alive with giddy butterflies, a sight irresistible to a gluttonous duck.

"*Buh-aaahk!*" Phil cried, waddling off to the feast.

This land, I thought, *this vast and fertile Kansas sea, once called the Great American Desert by people unable to see beyond the facts, is a truly beautiful place. What better setting can there be for the presentation of an awe-inspiring whale?*

All it needs is a little fixing up.

"Aren't you the artist?" A tourist — a middle-aged

woman with a telephoto camera — was addressing me.

"The artist?" I replied. "I don't know what you mean."

"Aren't you the one who's responsible for all this?"

"Oh," I said. "I guess I am."

"May I take your picture?" she asked politely. "With your creation? I think it's just magnificent."

I smiled uncomfortably into the lens.

"Thank you," she said. "You are not only very talented, you're also very kind."

I felt a peculiar feeling, an oil-and-water mixture of pride and unworthiness. It was like the time I'd gotten an A-plus on a paper my mother had helped me write.

After the first picture-taking tourist left, others approached me.

"My wife wanted me to ask if you'd be willing to speak to our children," a man explained. "They love to draw."

"May I have your autograph?" a teenager asked. "Just make it out to 'My friend Maisie.'"

"How did you decide to become a fossil artist?" a dark-haired woman inquired.

Before I could reply, her husband added, "Do you have more works planned?"

"Mr. Fossil Artist, could you step this way, please?" An elderly man with an instant camera beckoned with a liver-spotted hand. "Over here," he insisted. "Into the light."

The crowd surrounded me, their beaming faces all turned in my direction. I was quite literally the center of their attention.

Some roles in life we choose to play. Others are thrust upon us.

What was I to do? Sure, it's true that lying is an act to be avoided. But it's also a waste of time to argue with those who've made up their minds.

And what a terrific feeling!

Without further hesitation, I stepped to where the elderly man directed me, just a few feet from where I'd been standing — but light-years beyond the facts.

News 2 Me

Despite interruptions to pose for photographs, I managed to clean up the job site and complete a gravel pathway that circled the excavation. On a spot overlooking the grinning, rib-caged mosasaur's head, I set out a pair of wooden benches. Beside these, I placed a concrete birdbath. The result wasn't exactly beautiful, but it was better than before, and I was glad to have something to be responsible for.

Just being there made me feel older.

My father, of course, failed to see the change in me, but he couldn't help but notice the difference in our backyard. Whenever he looked outside, there were people admiring both the art and the artist.

"I hope you don't mind what's happening out there," I said, coming in for supper.

"Not at all," he replied. "It's opened up an opportunity."

"An opportunity?" I repeated.

"The State Museum has expressed renewed interest in our backyard," he replied.

"No!" I shouted. "You wouldn't!"

"Don't worry," he said. "I turned them down."

"Whew!" I responded. "Thank goodness."

"It's a negotiating tactic I learned years ago," he continued. "Never take the first offer. If people want something badly enough, they'll always go higher."

When it dawned on me what he was saying, I was so upset I couldn't speak.

I stared in disbelief.

How could this man be my father?

Knowing that I would regret anything I might say, I left the room to calm down. At times like these, it's good to have a pond video close at hand.

What a relaxing tape! I turned the sound down low, and within a few minutes slipped into that blissful space that lies somewhere between idle daydreams and real, honest-to-goodness dreams.

This is the place where Miss Whistle lives.

I tried to picture her face, but strangely, even though I'd seen her countless times, I had trouble remembering exactly what she looked like. I could close my eyes and visualize the freckles on her nose, but I could no longer simply order up a complete image of her face.

Why is that? I wondered. *Where do the mind's pictures go? Why, despite our wishes, do our memories flit away like butterflies? Is there a power you can summon to make them fixed, permanent, fossilized?*

My mind drifted like a runaway balloon. At some point, the video concluded, closing with a postcard-perfect picture of a finished pond and cascading waterfall. The video player automatically rewound, then it turned itself off with a soft, metallic click.

Perhaps it was this sound that awakened me.

Opening my eyes, I was surprised to find myself looking into the very same face that I can see in the mirror every day.

It was me, in my backyard!

Of course! When the video player went off, the television remained on. I was on TV!

I located the remote control and turned up the sound. The *News 2 Kansas* announcer was speaking.

"And so, failing to reach agreement with the landowner, the State Museum will ask the court to grant it custody of the Great Whale of Kansas," she said.

"What!" I exclaimed. "They're doing what?"

The announcer continued speaking during my outburst.

"And because a substantial portion of the whale was painted on public land, officials believe that the fossil artist placed his work into the public domain."

An aerial photograph of my fossil appeared on the screen. On top were written the words "Brewster Higley Memorial Park." On the bottom it read, "Homeowner's Backyard." A dotted line resembling a necklace around the whale's neck was labeled "Fenced Property Line."

I couldn't believe my very own eyes and ears!

"According to a spokesperson familiar with the fossil painting," the announcer said as Fossil Expert's broad face filled the television screen, "the State Museum hopes to develop the site into a major family attraction."

"This could be as big as the Wonderful World of Oz," Fossil Expert said, referring to a colossal Kansas theme park. "Maybe even bigger."

The picture flickered back to the announcer, who cheerfully changed the subject, saying, "Coming up next, has your dog gotten his new Kansas tags? This year, they're shaped like little bones!"

I clicked the television off, too stunned to speak.

Outside, a garbage truck rumbled down the street. From the basement, the washing machine whined as it spun a load of soggy clothes. In the kitchen, my mother clattered a butter knife against the sides of a nearly empty mayonnaise jar.

Eventually, with effort, I regained control of my

thoughts.

"That's *my* whale," I said.

The Fossil's Friend

Perhaps the reason nothing turns out the way you think it will is that nothing is exactly what you think it is. No matter how much you know, there's always something hidden underneath.

The State Museum, which didn't want anything to do with my fossil when they were sure it was a fake, couldn't wait to get their hands on it now that it was attracting crowds.

After a hundred million years of peace, my whale was doomed to becoming a state-operated sideshow freak — and it was all my fault!

Angry and confused, I rode my bike through Higley Park. Phil, the Solitary Duck, was sleeping on the banks of Higley Pond. How peaceful he seemed! Careful not to disturb him, I left half a pimiento cheese sandwich by his side and continued.

Not surprisingly, Tom White Cloud was alone in his bookstore.

"What I don't understand," I complained, "is how they can just come and take my fossil away from me. The biggest part of it is on *my* land."

"Governments have a way of making your land *their* land," Tom White Cloud replied. "It's called eminent domain. If you don't hand over your half of the fossil, they'll simply get a court to take it away from you."

"You're kidding!" I exclaimed. "They can't do that! It's private property!"

"Indians don't kid about governments taking land," Tom White Cloud responded. "It's something that governments do all the time. They confiscate land for parks, schools, streets — whatever they need — whenever they deem it to be in the public interest. And they don't need to win over a jury, either. All it takes is one sympathetic judge."

"That's not fair!" I cried.

"It depends on which side you're on," Tom White Cloud explained. "Unlike the time when America was 'settled,' as white people like to say, these days, the landowner is usually paid a fair price. But if you're the one whose property is being taken, even a fair price might not seem enough to make up for all your trouble."

"Can't anything be done to stop them?" I pleaded.

The thought of that majestic whale falling into the hands of those awful people made me sick inside.

The doorbell chimed and Miss Whistle walked in. Dressed in tan shorts and a black top, she'd obviously been spending her summer vacation in the sun. A riot of freckles was scattered like prairie stars across her forehead, arms, and shoulders.

"We were just discussing the pending fossil-napping," Tom White Cloud explained.

"A theme park," Miss Whistle said. "What a terrible idea!"

"Aw, come on now, Penny," Tom White Cloud said, giving me a wink. "Why shouldn't the State Museum run a theme park? Theme parks are fun!"

"Nonsense!" Miss Whistle retorted. "The notion that in order to teach you have to entertain all the senses is ridiculous! There's no opportunity for contemplation! Museums should be places that lead us to discover things — places where we can think about what we've discovered."

"I was just teasing, Penny," Tom White Cloud said. "I agree with you completely. Once again, the State Museum has gone too far."

"Isn't there some way to stop them?" I asked again.

Tom White Cloud frowned. "The hearing is next week," he said. "That's not much time."

"Surely, there's something that can be done," Miss Whistle implored. "After all, Tom, nothing is impossible."

"There is an old Indian trick I could try," Tom White Cloud replied, "but it's a long shot, and it'll have to come later. Right now, the best bet is to let people hear from the artist."

Miss Whistle looked at me as if everything had just been settled.

"Me?" I cried. "I don't know what to do."

"You're the whale's best friend," Tom White Cloud explained. "A lot of people will be interested in what you have to say."

"I think Tom's got something there," Miss Whistle agreed. "You should make a speech. It was our greatest president, Abraham Lincoln, who said, 'With public opinion on its side, nothing can fail.'"

"Lincoln got shot," I reminded her.

"It's a great idea," Tom White Cloud said. "We'll call a press conference. 'Tonight at six, the artist responds!'" he clowned, mimicking a *News 2 Kansas* announcer.

"Now, hold on!" I cried. "Maybe there's something we've overlooked."

What I didn't want to tell them was that I was afraid.

Ever since I was little, I've had this lump-throated, brow-sweating, knee-knocking fear of public speaking. And television? No way! When you're on TV, millions of people are watching every move you make. If you say something stupid, if your pants are unzipped, if you have a visible booger in your nose, you'll never live it down. Not ever.

Just as dinosaurs don't dance and fossils don't fly, TV was not for me. My answer could only be no, no, no, a thousand times, no!

I looked at the two of them looking back at me, my science teacher and my friend the bookstore owner, each with optimistic smiles, hopeful eyes, and, on one of them, sparkling red-gold hair. I knew at that moment how the mosasaur had felt the day he faced the Great Whale of Kansas.

Gulp!

"You're sure about this?" I asked weakly.

"It can't hurt," Tom White Cloud insisted.

"We'll be right behind you," Miss Whistle urged.

"All right," I whispered hoarsely. "But just this once."

Getting Ready

Kansas is a quirky sort of state, and Melville may well be its quirkiest town.

Something about this place attracts real individuals — independent, sometimes headstrong people who don't easily fit into groups. In pioneer times, such people were admired as rugged individualists. Nowadays, though, they're more likely to be thought of as strange.

Face it. People are more comfortable with people like themselves.

I was different.

Somehow, I had become a fossil artist, an illustrator of prehistoric wildlife whose canvas is that immense shelf of rock underneath the rich Kansas soil. That there had never been a fossil artist in Kansas before made no difference. There was one

110

now, it was believed, and I was it.

According to the plan hatched by Tom White Cloud and Miss Whistle, success depended on my making a speech on television, a one-boy performance for which I had less than two days to prepare. As far as I was concerned, this was like being told that I had less than forty-eight hours to live.

I was plenty scared, but I was also in a hurry. I studied up on fossils, prehistory, and especially whales. Tom White Cloud helped me find the books. Miss Whistle suggested that I organize my facts on index cards.

"It's the way professionals do it," she explained.

Since I had no index cards myself, I decided to search the private sanctum of my absent brother's bedroom. I sat at the desk where he'd studied in high school and rummaged through its drawers. I found a box of paper clips, dozens of dried-up ballpoint pens, and a small spiral notebook containing names and telephone numbers of girls. Index cards, however, were as scarce as hen's teeth.

My sister's room proved equally unrewarding. I found stacks of recorded music, rolled-up posters, and little cloth animals filled with plastic beans. Although I inspected every likely hiding place, there was not a single, solitary index card.

That was when I thought of my collection of Kansas postcards.

Some of these cards were useless, I realized. What

was I going to do with a photo of a concrete statue of Wild Bill Hickok or a picture of a prairie vole hiding underneath a log? And those dozens of studies of Kansas wheat, ranging from close-ups of ripening stalks to rippling, panoramic vistas, what good were they? Trains, owls, ropes, cowboy boots, fountains in a public square — it's not that I really needed any of these for sending to my friends.

I decided to keep my oldest cards and to use the rest to help save an ancient whale. Drawing the first one at random — a buffalo with her calf — I turned it over.

"Hello," I wrote. "Thank you for coming to see *Kansascetus humongous,* the Great Whale of Kansas."

The Press Conference

More than forty people had gathered in my backyard, including a crew from *News 2 Kansas*, neighbors, fossil visitors, and, of course, my parents, Tom White Cloud, and Miss Whistle.

At Tom White Cloud's suggestion, I stood on one of the benches to deliver my remarks, reading from the postcards I'd prepared.

"Hello," I said. "Thank you for coming to see *Kansascetus humongous,* the Great Whale of Kansas."

I paused to place that card behind the others, then, focusing my eyes at the top of the second card, I continued with my speech.

"When I first started this project, I didn't know what it would turn out to be. Frankly, I was expecting an ordinary dinosaur."

Unexpectedly, a few people chuckled at this confession, a response that caused me to lose my place. Not sure what to do, I retrieved the card I'd just put down and read it once again.

"Frankly, I was expecting an ordinary dinosaur," I repeated, "but now I'm glad that it's a whale. Here's why: Not so very long ago, while the Native Americans were being run off their lands, the whales were being chased from the seas. People weren't satisfied with simply killing whales or getting rid of Indians. No, for some strange reason, they felt they had to kill *all* the whales and Indians. And so it happened that after millions of years of doing quite well, both groups suddenly faced extinction."

From the front row, Tom White Cloud gave me a thumbs-up sign.

"If we stop to think about what happened," I continued, "we do so with shame. But mostly we don't think about it at all.

"Until *Kansascetus humongous* turned up, no whales had ever been found in Kansas, living, dead, or fossilized. Now there is one, and if I do say so myself, he's a beauty. Not only is he the biggest whale anybody's ever seen, he's also the only one of his kind.

"In other words, the Great Whale of Kansas is unique, with no siblings, no friends, and no companions other than his undigested lunch."

I paused so the audience could let this thought sink in. This was very nearly a mistake, for it gave my mind just enough time to imagine a mosasaur between two extremely large slices of bread. With effort, I fought off this distracting image.

"Today this whale is at a crossroads," I continued. "Some people want to exploit him, the way living whales once were processed for their oil and blubber and Indian lands were cut up into settlers' farms. They say this whale isn't what he's claimed to be, that he's simply a big decoration, and nothing more.

"Baloney! I say it's time to look beyond the facts we know to see the facts we don't."

Miss Whistle, who until now had been nervously gripping Tom White Cloud's hand, dropped it and clapped her hands together in approval.

"To my way of thinking," I told the crowd, "it's a matter of respect, respect not only for the living and the places they call home, but for the ancient dead as well. For if we don't care about the life that's gone before us, why should we be entrusted with the life that surrounds us now?"

Then, as I'd seen politicians do, and just as I'd practiced in front of the mirror, I pulled myself up to my full five-foot stature and shook my forefinger right at the TV camera.

"Leave this whale alone, I say!" I cried.

My unexpected gesture caused Tom White Cloud to burst into applause. Others, however, reacted differently. The cameraman from *News 2 Kansas,* thinking that I was about to take a swing at him, jumped backward in self-defense. This caused his heavy camera to slip from his shoulder, landing with a bone-cracking whump on his outstretched foot.

"*Arrrgh!*" he screamed.

His cry was no ordinary holler, but a frightening, inhuman sound, so blood curdling and primitive in its delivery that I dropped the remainder of my post-cards on which I'd copied the very best phrases of my speech.

Thus, the world was denied the pleasure of hearing me recite such venerable lines as "One of the most extraordinary creatures which the mutations of the globe have blotted out of existence" and "The eternal whale will still survive, and rearing upon the topmost crest of the equatorial flood, spout his frothed defiance to the skies."

Perhaps it's just as well.

When things eventually settled down, I concluded my remarks by ad-libbing, "Please protect the Great Whale of Kansas and his final resting place. Thanks a lot."

I stepped from my pedestal to polite applause, a

sound that remarkably is like the sound of the sea.

"How'd I do?" I asked my father, who'd recently changed sides on the issue of the whale's fate.

"You were fine," he said, somewhat unconvincingly. "It was a very thoughtful speech. The only trouble is, you went on for nearly ten minutes. On TV you have only about ten seconds to make your point."

"Really?" I replied, turning to sign an autograph for a kid about my age. "Only ten seconds?"

"Twenty if you're lucky," my father said. "Anyway, what's done is done. I wonder which part they'll choose."

The Evening News

My mother thought the press conference had gone exceptionally well. To celebrate my performance, she invited Tom White Cloud and Miss Whistle to stay for supper.

"He seemed so sincere," my mother bragged, passing a plateful of toasted cream cheese and olive sandwiches around the table. "And I liked the way he mixed Indians and whales together, while connecting prehistoric times, early settlers' days, and modern times, practically all in the same sentence."

"It was a very interesting approach," my father added. "Please pass the chips."

116

"What happens next?" I asked Tom White Cloud.

"Public opinion can influence a court's opinion," he explained. "Judges are people too, so when you appear in court next week, if we're lucky, you'll have Melville and the judge on your side."

"Good thinking," my father said.

"He's always thinking," Miss Whistle said proudly, as if Tom White Cloud were the star pupil in her class.

"*Hmmm,*" I said.

My mother returned from the kitchen with more sandwiches. "Did I miss something?" she asked.

"We were just talking about Tom," Miss Whistle said, squeezing his arm.

"It's time for the news," my father announced.

News 2 Kansas opened with a familiar fanfare and its usual stew of police stories, local commercials, and pictures of children playing. After nearly fifteen minutes of this, Tom White Cloud cracked, "I think I've seen this episode."

"Patience, Tom," Miss Whistle said. "Here it is now."

The picture changed from the *News 2 Kansas* newsroom to a slow panorama of the entire length of my fossil, starting at the whale's huge, bony head and lingering on the gobbled-up mosasaur with its grim, gaunt grin.

As the alarming picture slowly slid across the screen, the announcer said, "Where does a one-hundred-and-twenty-foot reptile-eating whale sit? If Melville's fossil artist has his way, it won't be in a theme park."

The picture cut back to the studio, where the announcer delivered her lines to the camera. "Today the Melville youngster asked the public to reject the State Museum's latest plan. Here's what he told *News 2 Kansas* earlier today."

Suddenly, there I was, standing on a bench with people all around me. On my face, I wore a stern expression as I read from the back of a postcard bearing the unmistakable image of a "jackalope."

"Frankly," my TV image recited, "I was expecting an ordinary dinosaur."

"Meanwhile," the announcer continued as Fossil Expert clumsily attempted to unfold a blueprint, "State Museum of Natural History officials say that when the theme park is completed, it will contain the largest gift shop in the entire state of Kansas."

Abruptly, the picture returned to the announcer, who proceeded with her cheery evening monologue: "Another dog has choked to death on his tag, the fifth such incident since new, bone-shaped tags were introduced."

"That's it?" I shouted, leaping from my chair. "That's all they used from my speech? 'Frankly, I was expecting an ordinary dinosaur'? I can't believe it! Why, it doesn't even make any sense! This is embarrassing!"

"You *looked* nice," my mother said.

"Yes," my father agreed. "But if you're going to go around saying things like 'Frankly, I was expecting an ordinary dinosaur,' would it hurt you to smile?"

Pennies from Heaven

The next morning I was awakened by a sound I could not identify.

I'd been dreaming about a solitary whale gliding gracefully through the silent, shadowy deep like a red-tailed hawk locked onto a soft prairie breeze, a huge, humpbacklike whale in prehistoric seas, its pectoral fins outspread like great, gray sails.

It was a peaceful, private, drifting sort of dream, and I was reluctant to let it fade away, but the unfamiliar sound of many conversations layered one upon the other, like shoppers bargaining in a busy market square, forced me to rise and investigate its source.

Perhaps I shouldn't mention this, but I don't sleep in pajamas. I haven't since I was a little kid. I just put on boxer shorts at night, right after my shower. And since there's only my mother and my father in the house with me, I often don't get dressed until after breakfast. So when I saw the crowds lined up to see my fossil, in my sleepiness I didn't stop to check my wardrobe before venturing outside.

There must have been five hundred people in my backyard that morning. They were moving in a line that snaked around the fossil past the birdbath, through the gate, and out into the park, ending in the parking lot beyond.

When the people saw me, they clapped, the way you'd clap for an actor at the conclusion of a play.

From my patio, I acknowledged their applause by waving to them. This made them applaud even louder.

What an extraordinary moment!

At last, I thought, *recognized by legions of fossil pilgrims! Celebrated with a spontaneous burst of public adoration! Why, I've made it! I'm famous! I'm a famous Kansan!*

The feeling was so incredible that even now I can't describe it, except to say how much I wish I hadn't been wearing only underwear.

Had I not been so blinded by momentary fame, I might also have noticed what else the visitors were doing. But famous people never see the forest for the trees, especially in Kansas, where so few trees grow.

It took my mother to point it out to me.

"They're putting money in the birdbath," she said. "Checks and dollar bills and pocket change, just like the collection plate in church. Isn't that nice?"

"Money?" I said, joining her at the breakfast room windows.

"It must have been that speech of yours," she

replied with pride. "I'll go tell your father. He'll be so pleased."

I watched the people filing past my fossil. One by one, they paused at the birdbath to leave a gift.

"Well, I'll be," I mused. "I wonder how much there is?"

My father appeared beside me and unexpectedly placed his hand on my shoulder.

"There's only one way to find out," he said softly.

The Hearing Begins

The Melville Courthouse is a two-story limestone-and-brick building whose history is more impressive than its appearance. In fact, its souvenir postcard is so crammed with historical details, there's no room left to write a message.

Erected in the 1830s at the starting point of the Lewis and Clark Expedition, the building was first used as a mission to the Kansa Indians. In 1855 it was the meeting place of the first Kansas territorial legislature. In the years that followed, it served as a Pony Express station, a Santa Fe Trail stagecoach stop, and an Atchison, Topeka & Santa Fe Railroad depot.

In the 1890s the world's largest salt deposit was discovered underneath the building, and it was promptly acquired by Morton Salt Company.

Abandoned in the 1930s, it was occupied for several years by a folk artist working in cement, during which time it suffered severe damage. After World War II, it was restored and remodeled, becoming an observatory, an aviation museum, a rodent zoo, the governor's mansion, a factory outlet store, the Greyhound Hall of Fame, and a Scandinavian bed-and-breakfast and birthplace of the famed Quattle-baum quintuplets. The building was acquired by the government in 1992.

What the Melville Courthouse could not be in size it had achieved through pedigree. Today it boasts the world's largest historical marker, a plaque as big as a cathedral door, weighing half a ton. People from all over Kansas come to be photographed in front of it.

Situated across the street from White Cloud Books in downtown Melville, the courthouse was as famil-iar a sight to me as the hedgeapple trees in my own backyard. Yet until the day of the hearing to deter-mine who would own the fossil, I had never set foot inside it. When at last I did, I found it crowded with Melvillians.

A brightly lit but windowless space, the courtroom was furnished with two large oak tables facing what appeared to be a pulpit flanked by flags, at which the Honorable T. Lawrence Quattlebaum soon would be presiding. Lined up behind the tables were four dozen long benches in two rows. All were filled with spectators.

Tom White Cloud and Miss Whistle sat in front with my parents and me. I didn't notice what my former science teacher was wearing that day, but I was disappointed to see that she'd developed a tiny pimple on her chin. Dominating the first row on the opposite side of the room were Fossil Expert and her ever-present assistants.

The lawyers sat at the tables, with papers, folders, and books stacked around them. The State Museum of Natural History was represented by the firm of Quattlebaum and Higley, Kansas's oldest, largest, and most expensive confederation of lawyers.

My fossil interests were being handled by my aunt Nan, my mother's sister from Great Plains who'd recently received her law degree from the University of Kansas. This was her first case, and I could tell that she was nervous. Every time someone entered the room, she stood up, thinking it was the judge.

Seated next to my aunt was a young man perhaps half her age, a department manager from the hobby shop, hired as an expert witness in sand art, the closest we could come to the subject of prehistoric limestone painting. His fee was being paid with money from the birdbath.

I took my seat beside my father. Behind me, everyone was talking at the same time in a steadily rising volume.

"Fifty dollars says the fossil art is gone by this time tomorrow," a woman wagered.

"Maybe he'll try something smaller next time," a man replied.

"Isn't that the science teacher sitting with the Indian from the bookstore?" someone whispered.

When Judge Quattlebaum appeared in the courtroom, he looked nothing like what I'd been expecting. Small, thin, red-faced, and bespectacled, with wispy white hair and a shadow of a mustache, he seemed old enough to have written Indian law. Everyone joined my aunt in standing as the elderly judge took his place at the bench.

"Who wants to go first?" he snapped.

"We're ready, Your Honor," said one of the lawyers from Quattlebaum and Higley. "But we need the lights turned down in order to show some slides."

"Well? Get the lights!" the judge barked to the bailiff, who jumped up to carry out the order.

The lawyer from Quattlebaum and Higley nodded to Judge Quattlebaum, who appeared to know him, and got right down to business.

The first slide was an aerial view of Higley Park and the adjacent houses — the one I'd seen on TV — with a white outline around the fossil and red-and-yellow markings showing the fence and property lines.

The lawyer from Quattlebaum and Higley began by explaining the position of the State Museum of Natural History. In a dull, scholarly monotone, he described a confusing legal picture consisting of "graffiti art," "abandoned objects," "fraudulent acts," "the public interest," "compensation for the state's losses," and "the need to protect public lands from encroachment."

His long-winded argument included many precedents and examples, each illustrated with additional slides and supported by thick stacks of paper.

There was no denying that Quattlebaum and Higley had done their homework. I was pretty sure they had me nailed to the side of the barn, so to speak, except that nobody seemed to understand what was being said, least of all Judge Quattlebaum. Pretty soon the old judge was fast asleep, as were many of the spectators. Undaunted, the lawyer from Quattlebaum and Higley pressed on with his presentation.

At noon the bailiff woke the judge, and the court recessed for lunch. Our team gathered at the sandwich shop in the basement.

"How do you think it's going?" I asked Aunt Nan.

"The State Museum seems to have all the facts on its side," she replied. "But so far, no one has applauded. That's a good sign."

"Keep your eye on the bailiff," a man at the next table said. "He's the key to winning this."

"How do you figure that?" Aunt Nan asked.

"The judge is asleep," he explained. "The bailiff will have to tell him what happened."

"And to think," my mother exclaimed, "this is the

same government that runs the schools!"

"Excuse me," interrupted a woman who was pushing a toddler in a stroller. "Could you autograph this napkin for my daughter? It's for when she grows up."

"Sure," I said.

No sooner had I responded to this fossil-artist fan than others began to form a line behind her. For the remainder of the lunch hour, I kept my mind off my troubles by signing autographs and posing for pictures by the soda pop machine.

"Shouldn't you be charging them something?" my father asked as we walked back to the courtroom. "I mean, why work for free?"

Court reconvened, and a rested Judge Quattlebaum looked at the two groups seated behind tables.

"Well," he said to my aunt, "let's get going. Ladies first!"

Puzzled, Aunt Nan looked across the aisle. The lawyers from Quattlebaum and Higley returned her gaze and shrugged. It seemed that the judge, having slept through the morning's proceedings, was under the impression the hearing was just beginning.

The lawyer from Quattlebaum and Higley stood up to try to straighten things out.

"Your Honor," he said, "I was planning to conclude my morning presentation with a short film about the many benefits of the proposed theme park."

126

"Sounds interesting," the judge said. "Now sit down!"

It was Aunt Nan's turn to shrug in apology to the lawyers from Quattlebaum and Higley as she stood up and nervously began to deliver her rehearsed remarks.

"Your Honor," she said, "this is an issue in which the ownership of a work of art is in dispute. My opponent believes that the state has the prevailing interest in this matter, but I rise to assert the fundamental rights of the artist. Throughout history, in every culture, artists have been awarded special status . . ."

As Aunt Nan gamely recited her speech, there was a noise in the back of the courtroom. I turned around to see a woman in a Kansas Parcel Service uniform talking to the bailiff and pointing in my direction. It was, of course, Mrs. Quattlebaum, Nathan's disagreeable mother, and she had a shoebox-size package in her hands.

I watched as the bailiff took it, shook it, sniffed it, and put his ear up against it, only to give it back to her with a nod of his head.

"I know this isn't your address," Mrs. Quattlebaum whispered when she arrived at our table, "but I figured I'd find you here. " She thrust a clipboard, a ballpoint pen, and the package at my science teacher's face.

"What've you got there, Penny?" Tom White

Cloud whispered.

"I'm not sure," Miss Whistle whispered in reply. "It looks like the lab results."

"Hey!" Judge Quattlebaum cried, smacking his gavel on the bench. "Maybe you folks would like to share your special delivery with the rest of us. Or are we making too much noise up here?"

"I'm very sorry, Your Honor," Miss Whistle said meekly.

"Well, you should be," Judge Quattlebaum snapped. "Now, what's in the box?"

"Go ahead, Penny," Tom White Cloud urged. "Tell the judge."

Relieved not to have to present her entire speech, Aunt Nan gathered up her papers and sat down.

Fossil Expert frowned as my science teacher rose.

"Your Honor," Miss Whistle said, "this is a sample taken from the discovery under discussion today."

From inside the box, Miss Whistle lifted out the fossil fragment that I'd given her on the last day of school.

"And this," she continued, holding up a bound document, "is the report on this sample from the National Testing Laboratory in Washington, D.C."

The spectators murmured at the mention of the nation's capital. Throughout history, messages from that distant city had often meant trouble for Kansans.

"I sent it off some time ago, hoping that by using modern scientific methods they could confirm what it is," Miss Whistle explained.

"So?" Judge Quattlebaum asked. "What is it?"

My science teacher brushed her red-gold hair from her face and scanned the report in her hand.

"Well," she replied, "according to this, it's not painted on, like everybody's been saying. It's definitely fossilized bone. Its carbon content suggests that it's approximately one hundred million years old."

The murmur suddenly became a dozen simultaneous conversations, among them, an annoyed Fossil Expert sputtering to her lawyers.

"Hush up!" Judge Quattlebaum barked.

When the noise subsided, Miss Whistle resumed reading from the report.

"Although no DNA material was found," Miss Whistle read, "the porosity and the cellular structure are consistent with that of whale bone."

Fossil Expert looked as if she were going to explode. Aunt Nan slumped into her chair. The expert witness from the hobby shop jumped to his feet, like a prairie dog popping from a hole. In every corner of the room, voices rose.

"Ha!" Mrs. Quattlebaum snorted. "I knew it! You people don't know facts from potatoes! That kid never made that thing! It's a dead whale as sure as the wind blows."

"Pipe down!" the judge demanded, rapping his

gavel on his desk. "Or I'll put every last one of you in jail!"

Turning to Miss Whistle, Judge Quattlebaum said, "Now, missy, you go sit while I take a look at that paper of yours."

Mumbling and muttering, the judge scanned the report from the National Testing Laboratory. At last, he turned the pages over and addressed the lawyers.

"These papers are the real McCoy," he announced. "Looks like the bones are too. I'm giving you folks until nine o'clock tomorrow morning to figure out what it is you're fighting over. This court is adjourned!"

The elderly judge smacked down his gavel and, with the assistance of his bailiff, slowly descended from his throne.

Up All Night

A house is very different after dark. It has different colors, different sounds, and different-size objects occupying its rooms. Even the distances, so familiar to your footsteps in the daylight, change at night, becoming longer, with twists and turns and dead ends that disappear by day.

I'm not usually allowed to stay up late, but on this night, when the whale-defending group gathered at my house in search of a last-ditch brainstorm, all curfews were swept into the shadows.

"Now what?" my father asked.

"Didn't you have something in mind?" I asked Tom White Cloud. "Some kind of old Indian trick?"

"It's not exactly a trick," he said. "I've seen it work in certain cases, although when it does, it rarely works for long."

"A shaman's magic spell?" I guessed. "A long-forgotten curse?"

"A long-forgotten promise, actually," Tom White Cloud replied. "I'm of the opinion that your fossil is on Indian land."

"That's impossible," Aunt Nan said. "The boundaries of the Indian reservations are clearly defined."

"It is unlikely, Tom," Miss Whistle agreed. "Higley Park is a public park, and their backyard is their private property."

"That may be so now," Tom White Cloud replied, "but in the 1850s it wasn't. During that time, three hundred and seventy separate treaties with indigenous Americans were signed by representatives of the United States government. Even though the government went on to break its word many, many times, the provisions of those treaties have never been invalidated."

"But if the Indians are entitled to the land around Higley Park," my mother asked, "couldn't they claim nearly all of Kansas, too?"

"Now that you mention it," Tom White Cloud

replied, "I suppose we could."

"It'll never work," my father insisted. "No one's going to hand over the deed to the state of Kansas just because of some hundred-and-fifty-year-old promises that everybody's forgotten. Not in a million years. I mean, face facts."

"When I look at the facts," Tom White Cloud replied, "I get discouraged. But when I look beyond the facts, I see possibilities that I never saw before."

"Well," Aunt Nan concluded, "I guess we'd better read the treaties. This could be a very long night."

A Whale in the Balance

The next day I understood why Judge Quattlebaum is so drowsy in the mornings. It's hard to keep your head up when you've gotten only half of your nightly sleep requirement.

Tom White Cloud and Miss Whistle had left sometime after one o'clock, which was about the time I went to bed. My aunt stayed over and slept in my sister's vacant room. Our group reassembled in the courthouse basement and pulled itself together over bagel sandwiches, orange juice, and coffee. A pale and tired Miss Whistle put on her makeup as my mother and Aunt Nan sorted papers.

Leaning against the wall was a map as big as a tabletop. The night before, my father had glued it to a sheet of plywood and cut it out all around the edges. He turned it around for Tom White Cloud to inspect.

"We need one more prop," Tom White Cloud decided. "A long nail mounted on a weighted base."

"I could try the Pioneer Spike and Spindle Museum," Miss Whistle said. "It's not far from here. I'm sure they'll let us borrow what we need — if they're open."

"Good idea," Tom White Cloud said. "But hurry. It's time for court to start."

We took our seats just as Judge Quattlebaum was taking his. "Where've you been?" he asked my aunt.

"Sorry, Your Honor," she replied.

"Think we can get going now?" the judge asked.

My aunt rose from her seat and began to speak, stepping away from the table and, I noticed, away from her notes as well.

"Your Honor," Aunt Nan began, "the gentlemen seated at the other table have offered many reasons for claiming my client's property. Now that we know we're dealing not with a man-made object, but with a bona fide, naturally occurring fossil, many of their arguments are moot. What they are left with is the contention that because a portion of the fossil was found on public land, the state has the authority to claim it all."

Aunt Nan paused and looked around the room. The spectators were respectfully silent.

"The state cites many legal decisions to support their position," she continued, "but what they've neglected to consider is that the land they say is public land may not be so at all, or, if it is, the object in dispute may be denied to the state forever."

A sound like waves crashing on a distant beach began to ripple through the crowded room. Everyone began whispering at once.

"What did she say?" I heard Mrs. Quattlebaum ask.

"She said Higley Park isn't public land," someone answered.

When my aunt resumed speaking, the noise died down.

"In 1856," Aunt Nan said, "a group of business-men, anxious to expand their profitable whaling operations, convinced government negotiators to insert a standard clause into all the treaties defining Indian Territory. If Your Honor will permit, I will read that clause now."

"Sure," Judge Quattlebaum said agreeably. "But speak up, will you?"

I surveyed the spectators. Fossil Expert was unwrapping a package of cream-filled sponge cakes. One of Fossil Expert's lawyers had his cell phone to his ear. Mrs. Quattlebaum was whispering to Nathan, who, on seeing me, waved. Out of respect to the court, I didn't wave back.

"Cedes in perpetuity," my aunt was reading,

"absolute control over all whales and whale habitat in that place defined as the point where a plane map of the states and its contiguous territories would balance, if it were of uniform thickness."

"What?" Mrs. Quattlebaum asked again.

"*Shhh!*" the man behind her said.

"In other words, Your Honor," Aunt Nan translated, "when the government took away the Native Americans' coastal whaling rights, it offered as compensation the exclusive right to hunt whales where no whales could possibly exist, far removed from any ocean, in the middle of what was known as the Great American Desert — the territory of Kansas. This was hardly a fair exchange, but it was typical of treaties at the time."

At that moment, Miss Whistle entered the courtroom carrying what looked like a dagger but was, in fact, an antique spike, a desk implement once used for holding pieces of paper.

"Now, if I may demonstrate," my aunt said as Miss Whistle placed the spike on the table and my father and Tom White Cloud lifted the big plywood map onto its sharpened tip, "the point where a plane map of uniform thickness balances is, as you can see, Melville, Kansas."

Judge Quattlebaum leaned so far over the bench that his bailiff, fearful that the judge might fall, clutched at the ends of his robes.

"And the point at which it balances in Melville,"

Aunt Nan continued, "is Brewster Higley Memorial Park!"

This time the spectators in the courtroom could hold it in no longer. Like water spilling over a dam, they came together to release wave after wave of pent-up oooohs and ahhhhs! Many expressed themselves while jumping up on benches in an impulsive gymnastic effort to see the plywood map of vintage America floating on a spike like a helium balloon drifting on a late summer breeze.

"If Your Honor will recall," my aunt continued, "yesterday it was established that the object in dispute is, in fact, the last remains of a once-living whale."

Aunt Nan retrieved a document from the corner of her table and handed it to the bailiff.

"Now, if it please Your Honor," she went on, "today I submit to this court a petition signed by Tom Macintosh, also known as Tom White Cloud, a descendant of the native Kansa tribe."

Tom White Cloud stood and nodded politely to the judge.

"Mr. Macintosh asks the court to award him the Melville whale and the land known as Higley Park," my aunt concluded, "plus the private backyard containing the majority of the fossil, with the government to compensate its owners at fair market value."

"What?" the lawyer from Quattlebaum and Higley said. "Now hold on just a minute!"

But few could hear his mild reaction over Fossil Expert's deafening shouts.

The Facts of Life

When Judge Quattlebaum ruled in Tom White Cloud's favor, everybody — including me — figured that the bookstore owner soon would open a museum.

What else would you do with a whale in Kansas?

Likewise, I thought that being on the winning side would increase my popularity. From where I sat, those logical assumptions felt like facts.

But facts are funny things. No matter how many you discover, there are always more you know you should have found. Like fossils hidden within fossils or postcards stacked fifty deep on a rack, facts never lose their power to surprise. On any given day, the facts we know can be replaced by those we don't.

Honestly, it wouldn't surprise me if after we're dead, we find out we didn't know anything at all.

After court adjourned, everyone crowded around Aunt Nan, shaking her hand and congratulating her on a fine presentation.

It was a much different story when people stopped to speak to me.

"Here," said a woman with a toddler in a stroller, handing me a napkin on which I'd signed my name.

"We don't want it anymore."

What's going on? I wondered.

Across the room, a kid my age tossed my picture into the trash.

An old man approached, claiming to have put ten dollars in the birdbath in my backyard.

"I thought you were a fossil artist," he said. "Now I find out you're just a museum keeper like everybody else in Kansas. I want my money back!"

Even Fossil Expert waddled over to weigh in.

"If the fossil is real," she sputtered, "then your fossil art is a fake! That makes you a fake!"

"But I never!" I protested.

My brain could not believe the news my ears were bringing it.

Aunt Nan passed by and smiled benevolently. Tom White Cloud and Miss Whistle left the courtroom holding hands. My parents were swallowed up by the crowd headed for the sandwich shop downstairs.

I closed my eyes and counted to ten. Perhaps I had misunderstood.

"So long, kid," said Mrs. Quattlebaum, pushing past. "Maybe the Indian will let you work for him."

At the doorway, her son, my classmate Nathan, turned around and waved goodbye.

For the longest time, I stood there waving back, stunned, silent, and empty of all thought — just a concrete statue forever waving in the center of an empty room.

From somewhere in the shadows came the raspy voice of old Judge Quattlebaum.

"Go on home!" he barked. "We're closed."

The Final Authority

I was concerned that something would fly into my father's mouth. It had fallen open in disbelief at a statement made by Tom White Cloud.

"But if you open a whale museum, you could be rich," my father pleaded with the owner of Melville's perpetually empty bookstore. "We all could."

"Many things are more important than making money," Tom White Cloud replied. "Foremost among these is being in harmony with the universe."

My father shook his head. "How about a very small museum?" he suggested. "Something tasteful, open only on weekends. Would that be a possibility?"

"The whale deserves better," Tom White Cloud insisted. "And, quite frankly, so does Melville."

Miss Whistle, dressed in tan slacks, a navy blazer, and, improbably, a beret, gazed lovingly at Tom White Cloud.

"But what about scientific understanding?" I asked. "What about the advancement of knowledge?"

"It's because of our knowledge that we make this

decision," Tom White Cloud replied. "It's because we understand what really matters."

"Oh," I said, still confused.

"Let me explain," Tom White Cloud said. "The Great Whale of Kansas is not the world's biggest ball of twine or the second biggest mechanized coal shovel. These ancient bones were once a living being. In size, and perhaps in other ways as well, this was the greatest creature ever to have lived. This is what you've been saying all along, correct?"

"Well, yes," I admitted.

"The Great Whale's spirit is still among us," Tom White Cloud continued. "By its presence, it commands us to give it honor and respect. This is not about money. It's about being at peace, about being at one with the Great Spirit — not just for the whale, but for all of us."

Fidgeting, I wondered, *Was I wrong to dig up the fossil in the first place?*

"There will be no museum," the Indian concluded. "The Great Whale of Kansas will be returned to the earth in a traditional native ceremony."

"Refreshments anyone?" my mother asked, entering the room with tiny sandwiches from which she'd carefully removed the crusts.

"What you're proposing sounds like catch-and-release fishing," my father observed, reaching for a snack. "Whenever you dig up a fossil, after you've finished looking at it, you put it back the way you found it. I guess that makes sense."

"Thank you," Tom White Cloud said. "I knew you'd understand."

The Valley of the Dry Bones

You never know who's going to show up for a funeral. When there's absolutely no doubt it's the final sendoff, funerals attract friends and enemies alike.

Native Americans from all across Kansas responded to the call, as did everybody who's anybody in Melville — the mayor of Melville, the principal of Melville Elementary School, the president of Melville State Bank, and Judge T. Lawrence Quattlebaum, who dozed in a purple folding chair by the cooking pots. Even Fossil Expert showed up, at least for some of it. As it turned out, what Tom White Cloud had in mind for the Great Whale of Kansas was a nonstop Native American service running four consecutive days and nights.

"Why four days?" I asked him beneath a crescent moon while chowing down on a slice of hot frybread and a bowlful of thick, steaming corn-and-beef stew.

"That's how long the spirit lingers," he explained.

"Well, I mean no disrespect," I replied, "but it seems to me you've missed the deadline by roughly a hundred million years."

The War Mothers were given the place of honor, in the first row, at the edge of the excavation. These are the oldest women in the tribe. They're so old, they can recall the days of hardship brought on by the white invaders. Clustered together, chattering, and singing hymns in a native dialect, there wasn't a single one of them under the age of ninety.

The War Mothers maintained a vigil over the whale's earthly remains, keeping his spirit company and a fire burning twenty-four hours day.

The War Mothers were also in charge of the veil that protected the deceased from casual view. Whenever someone came to pay respects, the War Mothers carefully removed it. Although the veil was fashioned from lightweight fishing net, this still was no easy task, given that the deceased was one hundred and twenty feet long. But the War Mothers had seen tougher duty over the years, so with much grunting, groaning, and tugging, they opened and closed this final curtain hour after hour, day after day, seemingly without sleeping.

A team of medicine men took turns praying for the whale. Like the War Mothers, the medicine men spoke in dialect, which from time to time they would translate, almost as an afterthought.

"*Waconda, he husheme,*" they repeated quietly. "Grandfather, pity me. *Waconda, he husheme.* Lord, have mercy on me."

I was very surprised to see that many of the native

people were crying. The loss of one, I gathered, no matter how distant in time and species, was in some ways the death of all.

Each of the Native Americans brought blankets, shawls, and other handmade gifts to share with the deceased. Recognizing me as the whale's next of kin, they placed these offerings at my feet, shook my hand, and in English and in dialect expressed their sorrow.

"It wasn't that long ago you would have received gifts of horses and ponies," Tom White Cloud whispered. "But don't get too attached. At the end of the ceremony, you'll have to give everything back."

I gave him a questioning look.

"It's the custom," he explained.

The native people also brought great quantities of food, which they prepared over open fires throughout the day and night.

"When the spirit is around," Tom White Cloud explained, "everyone must eat. The more you eat, the more you honor the spirit. If you do not eat, you insult the spirit."

I gave the spirit no cause to complain. I consumed a dozen meals a day for four days without letup. Frybread, biscuits, sausage, gravy, soup, stew, tea, coffee — anything that can be cooked in a pot. And not once did a sandwich dare to show its face.

After two days and nights of eating, mourning, talking, napping, and praying for the spirit of the deceased, a new medicine man appeared who apparently outranked the other medicine men. A small person with a tanned, deeply lined face, he carried himself with great dignity. He also carried a leather bag covered with ribbon in the shape of lightning bolts. From inside the bag, he extracted a pinch of what looked like tea.

"*Waconda, he husheme,*" the head medicine man said as he sprinkled the substance into the War Mothers' fire. A tiny puff of white smoke went up, followed by a faint woody aroma.

"That's cedar," Tom White Cloud explained. "Dried, crumbled branches of the cedar tree."

Speaking first in dialect, then in abbreviated translation, the head medicine man addressed the mourners.

"The cedar tree," he said, "stands for hope. Even in a drought or snowstorm, it is green. Thus, the cedar comforts us. It is good medicine. It chases the bad spirits away."

Another man scooped a shovelful of coals from the War Mothers' fire. Retrieving a handful of dried cedar from his bag, the head medicine man spoke some Indian words and tossed the cedar into the coals. Immediately, a thick cloud of white pungent smoke arose. The head medicine man reached to the top of his head, patted his braided hair, then suddenly gave a stricken look. In a soft but anxious voice, he spoke in native dialect to his assistant.

"What's going on?" I asked Tom White Cloud.

"He can't find his eagle feather," Tom White Cloud replied. "He needs it to perform the ceremony. It's a critical element."

The head medicine man now addressed the mourners. Some of them looked around with obvious concern. Others shook their heads in disappointment. Judge Quattlebaum continued sleeping.

"Now what?" I asked.

"He's asking to borrow an eagle feather," Tom White Cloud said, "but no one has one."

"There must be a thousand Native Americans here," I said in disbelief. "Are you telling me there's not a single eagle feather among them?"

"Times have changed," Tom White Cloud replied. "For eagles as well as Indians."

Suddenly, I had an idea.

"Don't go away," I said, sprinting from the safety of the funeral's firelight into the empty darkness of Higley Park.

It's a good thing I knew the black asphalt pathway blindfolded, because the light from the weak grimace of a moon was enough to illuminate only pale, reflective colors, such as white, wet objects — objects like a duck dozing at the edge of Higley Pond.

"Sorry, Phil," I apologized, plucking a six-inch feather from the sleeping waterfowl's tail. "It's for a good cause."

"*Buh-aaahk,*" Phil muttered.

The head medicine man seemed amused by my contribution, but he accepted it with native words of thanks.

"Eagle fathers are considerably larger," Tom White Cloud whispered. "But under the circumstances, it seems your duck feather will do."

The head medicine man climbed down into the pit. Speaking sacred words, he touched the feather to the fossil. Back on top, he again charged the coals with cedar and, using the duck feather as a wand, wafted the holy smoke into the Great Whale's grave.

With hands as gnarled as hedgeapple branches, the War Mothers reached into the smoke as it billowed by, bathing their faces and their hair in the good medicine.

"Waconda, he husheme," they cried.

The head medicine man delivered the healing magic to each mourner. One by one, he blessed us, tapping us with the feather from Phil, the Solitary Duck, scooping up the cedar smoke, and swirling it around our heads.

My eyes watered and shut involuntarily. When I opened them, everything looked different from before. People's faces seemed softer, kinder, and more alike in the flickering night-light.

Tom White Cloud and Miss Whistle comforted the War Mothers. Nathan Quattlebaum and his mother stood arm in arm. The head medicine man approached Fossil Expert. The sizable spokesperson for the State Museum of Natural History knelt before the little gnomelike Indian. Waving Phil's feather above Fossil Expert's bowed head, the head medicine man covered my summer enemy in a blue, translucent haze.

That was when the strange thing happened.

Struck on the outside with a sudden, unexplained chill, inside I felt my heart strangely warmed. Fossil Expert no longer looked ugly and ungainly to me. She had become a creature freed from the limitations of land. Suddenly, she possessed the sleek beauty of a whale in command of earth's endless seas, power and grace united in one extraordinary being — a being now humbling herself in the face of life's greatest mystery.

I had been wrong.

From across Kansas, people had come together in one spirit to celebrate the life and mourn the death of the biggest creature ever to have lived. Yet time and time again, I'd dismissed Fossil Expert simply because of her unusual size.

Talk about jumping to conclusions!

"*Waconda, he husheme,*" I said out loud.

"It's all right," my father replied, putting his arm all the way around me.

With each of the mourners blessed, all voices were stilled. The night became calm. Time was without end. A clean, pure, and invigorating presence rose from the excavation and filled the air like light, but it was not light, sweeping over the mourners like music, but it was not music.

Never had I felt so wonderful.

The assistant with the shovelful of coals stood in front of the Great Whale's final resting place. The head medicine man blessed him, blessed himself, and together they returned the coals to the War Mothers' fire.

Final Thoughts

Things never turn out the way you think they will, but sometimes that's okay.

I finally got my backyard pond, my own private water-garden retreat. It's everything the video promised it would be — tranquil, soothing, perfect for reflection, and not bad just for hanging out and doing nothing much at all.

My pond is not as big as the pond in Higley Park, of course, but it's got the best thing that Higley Pond ever had. The day after I filled my pond with water, Phil, the Solitary Duck, moved in.

Sitting here watching the south wind fluff his bright white feathers, I wonder if maybe he doesn't have the right idea about lots of things, paddling around by himself, happy to accept whatever sandwiches may come his way. In a land where museums, Quattlebaums, and new opportunities are as plentiful as fossils, I realized, who needs to waste time wishing for Miss Whistle? She's much too old for me, and even if she weren't, she's far too preoccupied with her appearance — especially her clothes.

I guess I must have been pretty lonely.

It's hard to insert yourself into other people's lives.

I apologized to my father for causing his accident at the pit. He apologized to me for not helping with my fossil. We talked for a long time, saying whatever popped into our heads while skipping stones over the surface of my new pond.

I've learned that very often situations aren't what they seem. If you keep digging, or simply wait, one set of facts almost always will yield to another.

In Kansas, I guess, it's easier to get through life if you have a good imagination.

Underneath everything lies the Great Whale of Kansas.

One person's exaggeration is another person's hope.

One boy's fossil sketch is a whole town's art.

The Melville City Council adopted my pen-and-ink drawing of the mosasaur within the whale as the city's official symbol. Something about the way the reptile is spending eternity in the middle of a whale caught the lawmakers' eye, reminding them of how Melville feels, stuck in the dead center of Kansas, which is the belly of America.

Next week, emblazoned in the center of the new

Melville flag, my illustration will be raised to the top of City Hall. The ceremony will be carried live on *News 2 Kansas*.

As the artist, I'm expected to make a speech.

Souvenir postcards of my original design are on sale at the drugstore, priced at twenty-five cents each or five for a dollar. Autographed copies are available upon request, at no extra charge.